100 Ideas for Secondary Teachers:

Outstanding RE Lessons

Andy Lewis

BLOOMSBURY EDUCATION

LONDON OXFORD NEW YORK NEW DELHI SYDNEY

BLOOMSBURY EDUCATION
Bloomsbury Publishing Plc
50 Bedford Square, London, WC1B 3DP, UK

BLOOMSBURY, BLOOMSBURY EDUCATION and the Diana logo are
trademarks of Bloomsbury Publishing Plc

First published in Great Britain, 2020

A catalogue record for this book is available from the British Library

ISBN: PB: 978-1-4729-7242-2; ePDF: 978-1-4729-7241-5;
ePub: 978-1-4729-7243-9

4 6 8 10 9 7 5 3 (paperback)

Typeset by Newgen KnowledgeWorks Pvt. Ltd., Chennai, India
Printed and bound in the UK by CPI Group (UK) Ltd, Croydon CR0 4YY

To find out more about our authors and books visit
www.bloomsbury.com and sign up for our newsletters

Contents

Acknowledgements

A few thank yous and acknowledgements:

- To my own RE teachers: Mr Pegler, Mrs Smith, Mrs Thomas and Ms Hayden – you inspired me to be an RE teacher.
- To the RE department at Homerton College and the Faculty of Education, University of Cambridge: Janet Scott, Mary Earl and Peter Mitchell – you trained me to be an RE teacher.
- To all my colleagues past and present, but particularly my former subject leaders: Viv Moore at St John Payne, Chelmsford and Pauline Treacy at Sacred Heart of Mary Girls' School, Upminster – you helped and encouraged me to become a subject leader of RE.
- A huge thanks also to my current team at St Bonaventure's. It is a genuine pleasure to work with you all: Axel, Daniella, Áine, Liam, Gary and Chris – and to Graham and Vivienne, my line managers who keep pushing me to be even better as an RE teacher and curriculum leader.

This book would be impossible without a number of people who contributed ideas, offered encouragement, gave constructive criticism and kept me going when it got tough! I am really grateful – 100 is a really big number of ideas to come up with. You'll see some of these names included in the ideas, while some of them worked behind the scenes. You have been brilliant, thank you.

In alphabetical order...
Waqar Ahmedi, Bob Bowie, Adam Boxer, Claire Clinton, Dawn Cox, Matthew Dell, Claire Doherty, Abbey Elton, James Holt, Doug Lemov, Nikki McGee, Neil McKain, Matt Pinkett, David Rogers, Philip Robinson, Arabella Saunders, Mark Shepstone, Anthony Towey, and A. J. Smith.

Thank you to the RE online communities: Save RE, RE Teachers Forum, #REChatUK and @TeamRE_UK – you are a valuable support for *all* RE teachers, and have helped and inspired me over the years.

Thank you to the team at Bloomsbury who had faith in me to deliver this book, and have helped at every step of the way. Chloe, Hannah and Sarah – you have been fantastic.

A final thanks to my amazing wife Emily who lets me stay up late at night to write (even on holiday!), and my two fantastic boys, Tommy and Joseph, who try their very best not to mess up Daddy's 'work'. I love you all so much.

Introduction

RE teachers are a quite incredible group of people. They often demonstrate such a deep passion for their subject that their students become co-defenders and co-promoters of RE both within and beyond the school. They want their students to understand the world, but also to understand something of themselves.

However, many find themselves in tough circumstances, without the support and resources they need. It is not unusual for the RE teacher to be the only subject specialist, expected to deliver the subject in ways unlike any other curriculum area. They can also find RE diluted into an amalgamation of other subjects, or taught just as drop-down days. It can be tough being an RE teacher, but RE teachers also want to help and support one another as a genuine community.

The subject also has an identity crisis. 'Two Jews, three opinions' says the Jewish proverb, and the world of RE is very similar. There are many areas of discussion and debate as the relatively new subject reforms, considers name changes, reviews its contributing disciplines, and incorporates other subject areas.

The key areas of debate that the RE teacher needs to consider are:

- **Depth versus breadth:** how many religions or non-religious worldviews is it possible to study in the designated curriculum time? Do you need a balance between Abrahamic and Dharmic faiths?
- **Competing disciplines:** philosophy, sociology, theology, history... this affects not only *what* but also *how* RE is taught!
- **Relevance and engagement:** what is the opportunity cost of certain activities? Have entertainment and fun influenced activities more than learning?
- **Purpose and aims:** what are we trying to achieve in RE lessons? Do we have a common definition of 'religious literacy'?

I also believe that our subject is potentially the most important subject our students need as they navigate their futures; the principles of philosophy and ethics, alongside an understanding of the role of religion in history, politics and daily life (whatever their personal faith), are going to be vital. The advancement of technology, science and medicine will need to be carefully managed by people able to ask and answer the question, 'Just because we can, does it mean we should?' RE might just help them with that.

I hope this book is a source of inspiration, but I acknowledge that it doesn't have all the answers. Getting the RE curriculum right is perhaps the most important job of the RE teacher: the *what* or the substance. We then need to look at the *how*, and how this fits in with the various disciplines found in RE.

Parts 1 to 3 of this book are focused around understanding the background to the subject, curriculum planning and raising the profile of the subject. Parts 4 to 6 deal with the delivery of some specific topics and areas of RE. Parts 7 and 8 look at different resources, as well as ways of making the subject authentically relevant and engaging. Finally, parts 9 to 11 look at key skills, assessment and exam skills.

Don't start with the activity and work backwards; establish what you want the students to know, or be able to do, and then use this book, possibly, to help you do that. It may get you to rethink some of your established practices, or consider doing things a little differently next time. Some ideas will be useful to you; some might not be.

I wrote this book as I wanted to make a positive and practical contribution to Team RE. Despite our differences of opinion on certain things, we all want better RE in every school. There are many debates that might happen about RE outside the classroom, but what goes on inside it on a daily basis is really the most important thing. I've tried to talk to as many RE teachers as I can about what they wanted, needed and felt would be useful. This book hasn't just come from me; it's a collection of many good ideas, from many great teachers.

I do hope this book helps even in a small way.

How to use this book

This book includes quick, easy and practical ideas for you to dip in and out of to help you deliver truly outstanding RE lessons.

Each idea includes:

- a catchy title, easy to refer to and share with your colleagues
- an interesting quote linked to the idea
- a summary of the idea in bold, making it easy to flick through the book and identify an idea you want to use at a glance
- a step-by-step guide to implementing the idea.

Each idea also includes one or more of the following:

Teaching tip

Practical tips and advice for how and how not to run the activity or put the idea into practice.

Taking it further

Ideas and advice for how to extend the idea or develop it further.

Bonus idea ★

There are 18 bonus ideas in this book that are extra-exciting, extra-original and extra-interesting.

Share how you use these ideas and find out what other practitioners have done using **#100ideas**.

The background to RE

Part 1

What is RE?

'Before I began to teach the subject, I needed to work out exactly what it is!'

Students, parents, teachers and school leaders all make assumptions about RE and what it is. A basic understanding of the history of the subject can help the RE teacher understand why we are where we are today.

Teaching tip

Further reading: *Teaching Religion* by Terence Copley (University of Exeter Press, 2008), which covers the period 1944 to 2008 in detail.

Here is a brief outline of how the subject has developed:

1944–c.1960: the subject was known as 'Religious Instruction' and also involved the provision of collective worship. It was taught non-denominationally, but faith schools could undertake faith-based teaching. Parents could withdraw their children, and teachers could withdraw from teaching it, but ultimately the main aim was to create a post-war society based on Christian values.

c.1960–c.1970: research found students were confused by what they were learning and that they would be better engaged with issue-based learning. This would make religion more relevant to them. There was far less Bible study, as RE distanced itself from Sunday School approaches.

c.1970–1988: some schools began to teach Humanism as part of RE (which caused controversy), as well as world religions (far less controversial). Phenomenology became a more popular approach thanks to Ninian Smart, and confessional approaches were seen negatively by many teachers in community schools.

1988–2004: the 1988 Education Reform Act officially renamed the subject as 'Religious Education', and required the subject to cover the principal religions of the UK, but reflecting that they are 'in the main, Christian'. Content was to be determined locally, with each Local Education Authority producing their own locally agreed syllabus (LAS). Withdrawal rights were kept, faith schools retained their right to faith-based teaching, and the Cowper-Temple clause continued ensuring teaching outside faith schools was non-denominational. Crucially, RE was left outside the new National Curriculum but was part of the 'basic' curriculum.

2004–2015: *The Non-Statutory National Framework for RE* (2004) was published by the Qualifications and Curriculum Authority and the Department for Education and Skills and influenced many locally agreed syllabuses. Critical RE emerged, as did merges with citizenship and PSHE. The academy and free-school programmes allowed schools to opt out of their LAS, but they still had to follow an agreed syllabus.

2015–present: 2015 saw a number of reports launched on the current state of RE: does it need a new name? A new legal status? A new purpose? A new approach? See reports such as *RE for All* and *A New Settlement: Religion and Belief in Schools*. This then led to a two-year commission, which in 2018 published *Religion and Worldviews: The Way Forward. A National Plan for RE*, which answered yes to most of the above questions. It put forward 11 recommendations, which were widely supported by the RE community.

Summary

- RE remains legally compulsory for all students until they leave education.
- Broadly speaking, Christian collective worship remains legally compulsory for all schools.
- The two laws above are frequently ignored by schools.
- RE remains locally determined.
- The rights of withdrawal from RE remain.
- Faith schools can follow their own RE syllabuses and provide their own collective worship.

Taking it further

Consider the history of RE within your own school: has it changed significantly in recent history? Why did those changes take place? What is the future for RE in your school?

3

IDEA 2

The pedagogy of RE

'Everything works somewhere, and nothing works everywhere.'
(*Dylan Wiliam*)

Considering the different possible pedagogies in RE will make teachers more aware of their role within the subject.

Teaching tip

Most RE teachers will use a mixture of pedagogies, rather than be total advocates of just one approach.

In simple terms, 'pedagogy' means the teaching method used. Different teachers will have their own rationale and perceived purpose of the subject, while the students and their context (particularly their type of school) will also have an impact.

Some of the main pedagogies (in chronological order)

- **Faith nurture:** this is an approach put forward by Thomas Groome, and many see schools with a religious character as delivering RE in this way. This is also what many see RE's former model of RI (Religious Instruction) to be.
- **Phenomenology:** this is the approach often linked to Ninian Smart and his work in the late 1960s, whereby religions were studied as a series of phenomena: stories, rituals, teachings and values. The aim was objectivity and empathy.
- **Interpretive:** this approach is a way of trying to get students to interact with ways of life different to their own, often through the stories of believers. Robert Jackson's work is often linked to this approach.
- **Human development:** Michael Grimmitt's work focuses on 'making meaning' and is associated with AT2 (attainment target 2: 'learning from'). Learning and tasks are often linked to the personal development of students.

4

- **Experiential:** David Hay and John Hammond's approach to RE focuses on the spiritual development of students. As well as helping them learn about RE, it allows for the development of emotions, feelings and a sense of identity within the subject.
- **Concept cracking:** this is an approach usually associated with the teaching of Christianity and is based on the work of Trevor Cooling. It moves beyond the phenomena to incorporate the personal or communal experience of believers.
- **Critical realism:** Andrew and Angela Wright's approach focuses on the reality of religions and beliefs, while maintaining a critical and enquiring position. It relies on theological and philosophical questioning.
- **Conceptual enquiry:** this is a way of conducting a systematic investigation into the concepts of religion and belief. Clive Erricker's work can be seen as a philosophical approach to the subject with a five-step enquiry model. It is sometimes seen as a 'deconstructivist approach'.

Taking it further

Read more information on these approaches, including their advantages and disadvantages at www.natre.org.uk/primary/teaching-re/methods-of-teaching-re-1.

Which is best?

All approaches have value and use, and have worked in certain settings. What seems important is that the RE teacher considers their own position. This will naturally take into consideration many different factors, including intellectual influence, personal belief and/or faith, the curriculum used in a particular school, the context in which you teach and the needs of your pupils.

What's next?

The subject continues to develop and potentially change. As a relatively 'young' subject, the last 50 years have seen huge shifts in the approaches and pedagogies used in RE. However, there are equally many advocates within RE of the existing approaches.

RE vs collective worship

'Why am I expected to lead collective worship?'

The ability to deliver a short, powerful and memorable message to a large group of students is a skill well worth developing.

Section 70 of the School Standards and Framework Act 1998 states that all pupils in maintained schools in England and Wales must take part in a daily act of collective worship 'of a broadly Christian character', unless pupils have been withdrawn. The reality is that in many schools this no longer takes place, and Ofsted have not reported on it for a significant period of time.

In *Religious Education and Collective Worship* (1994), the Department for Education's stated aim for collective worship is for schools to: 'provide the opportunity for pupils to worship God, to consider spiritual and moral issues and to explore their own beliefs; to encourage participation and response, whether through active involvement in the presentation of worship or through listening to and joining in the worship offered; and to develop community spirit, promote a common ethos and shared values, and reinforce positive attitudes'.

The spiritual and moral elements have often seen collective worship, namely assemblies, come under the remit of the RE department. Yet does this confuse teaching about religion with encouraging students to be religious?

An RE teacher in a school with a religious character may well expect to be involved in collective worship, but if you work in any other kind of school, it is worth looking carefully at what is being provided. A meeting with a senior staff member asking about the aims of the collective act can be beneficial.

Bonus idea ★

Students are often keen to help deliver assemblies. If you are responsible for assemblies, use the expertise and enthusiasm of those you teach!

RE CPD

'How do I become a better RE teacher?'

How to become a better RE teacher can be a really pertinent question for small departments, especially if you are the only RE specialist in the school.

Here are some CPD ideas:

NATRE-affiliated local groups: The National Association of Teachers of RE (NATRE) helps to support over 260 local network groups in the UK, Hong Kong and Cyprus. The group leader is sent a termly newsletter and CPD presentation to distribute. These are then discussed at the local meeting. Find out if there is an existing local group via the NATRE website.

Twitter: useful accounts to start following are @TeamRE_UK, @NATREupdate and @reonline_tweets. There is a monthly Twitter chat hosted by NATRE using the hashtag #REChatUK; it currently meets virtually on the first Monday of the month at 8 pm for an hour.

Facebook: the biggest Facebook group is called 'Save RE', set up initially in response to RE's exclusion from the EBacc. It has well over 7,000 members. There are also smaller groups such as 'RE Teachers Forum', as well as exam-board specific groups.

Events: there is no substitute for meeting other real-life RE teachers! The biggest annual event is the NATRE conference called 'Strictly RE', which is usually held in January. There are many other events too that you can find out about by keeping an eye out on social media and joining a NATRE local group.

Online courses: sites such as www.futurelearn.com provide lots of free online courses to help enhance subject knowledge.

> **Teaching tip**
>
> Consider if you want to use your personal social media accounts to network or whether it would be beneficial to set up a separate 'professional' account. This can also help with work/life balance!

> **Taking it further**
>
> If there is no NATRE local group near you... start one up! Just three or four RE teachers from a local area can meet termly to discuss and share ideas.

Complete a Farmington Scholarship

'Much of the education in schools seems to be based on the *what* and the *how* of learning. Farmington – for me – addresses and validates the *who* and the *why*.' (*Heather Torren*)

Farmington Scholarships are for teachers of religious education and other associated subjects. Scholars can study any aspect of religious education, but it is preferred if work can be seen to be of direct value to the teaching of RE in schools.

Teaching tip

Is there a research project that you can identify within your department that you do not have the time or resources to complete? Why not consider a Farmington Scholarship to give yourself the opportunity to complete it?

The Farmington Institute in Oxford provides a number of scholarships each year to RE teachers. The scholarship covers tuition fees, local travel and a contribution towards cover costs. Scholars can then choose to complete their scholarship during a block of up to eight weeks or day release up to 30 days in the academic year.

Before beginning, scholars send a study plan for approval and then present their work to their partner university and/or school, and then again at the annual Farmington Conference. Once they have completed their research, they summarise it in a final report.

Completing a Farmington Scholarship also allows you to attend all future conferences while you are involved in teaching RE, enabling you to be part of a network of RE teachers who are committed to improving their own practice and that of others.

Bonus idea ★

The reports written by previous scholars are available to request online from www.farmington.ac.uk.

Most reports fit into one of the following categories: moral and ethical issues, philosophy and spirituality, science and religion, teaching and training, theology and doctrine, and world religions (although over half are in the 'teaching and training' category).

The name of RE

'I want to rebrand my department to make it sound more appealing to students and parents!'

Rebranding can be a success, but it is always important to consider the aims of a name change.

The name chosen for a department will often tell you something about the approach of the department ('Philosophy and Ethics'), or the way in which the subject links to other curriculum areas ('Citizenship, PSHE and Religion'). It may tell you something of the academic backgrounds or aspirations of the team ('Theology' or 'Divinity'). It is impossible to say that any names are bad – apart from maybe 'Citizenship, Religion and Philosophy' (abbreviated to CRaP)!

Two key names for the subject are:

- **Religious Education:** the legal name and what schools are required to teach to all students in full-time education. It is also the internationally recognised name for the subject.
- **Religious Studies:** the name of the GCSE and A level.

'Religion and worldviews' is another name being used more frequently since the Commission on RE in 2018. However, the list of possible names is very long, including for example: ER (Ethics and Religion), RPE (Religion, Philosophy and Ethics) and DP (Divinity and Philosophy).

To change or not?

It is always important to consider the aims of a rebrand. Will it be just the name that changes? Sometimes focusing on the teaching and learning that goes on can be enough to change the subject's perception without a rebranding.

Taking it further

It is worth knowing the history of names in RE, such as its beginnings as Religious Instruction (RI). The name indicates a very different approach!

RE associations

'Who or what can I join for professional support?'

RE teachers will often seek out CPD in various ways, but by joining a subject association you will find a whole range of other opportunities: free resources, conferences, networking opportunities, and so on.

You might want to think about joining one or more of the associations listed below.

- **NATRE:** The National Association of Teachers of RE. Membership is popular for many RE teachers and departments due to the resources and level of support provided. It is supported by RE Today (a publishing house and CPD provider). Joining the Executive can provide opportunities to support and shape RE nationally.
- **REC:** The Religious Education Council. Membership is for organisations rather than individuals. You could subscribe to their email newsletters, which contain news from the REC and its member organisations.
- **NASACRE:** The National Association of Standing Advisory Councils on Religious Education, which supports and represents SACREs (SACRE stands for Standing Advisory Council on Religious Education). Membership is usually for people who are involved in SACREs who want to get involved at a national level. Many teachers like to get involved with their SACRE as it is useful for networking locally, or for finding speakers or local places of worship to visit.
- **AREIAC:** The Association of RE Inspectors, Advisers and Consultants. Membership is usually for RE professionals who are inspectors, advisors and consultants.

- **AULRE:** The Association of University Lecturers in Religion and Education. Membership is usually for those working in higher education in RE, including initial teacher education (ITE).

Religion- and belief-specific groups

- **ACT:** The Association of Christian Teachers. Membership is open to all Christians who work in education.
- **CATSC:** The Catholic Association of Teachers, Schools and Colleges. Membership is open to Catholics in education, but is usually institutional rather than individual.
- **ATCRE:** The Association of Teachers of Catholic RE. Membership is open to anyone teaching Catholic RE.
- **JTA:** The Jewish Teachers' Association. Membership is open to all Jewish people working in education.
- **MTA:** The Muslim Teachers' Association. Membership is open to all Muslims working in education.
- **Humanist Teachers:** membership is open to all working in education.

Taking it further

Why not find out if there is a NATRE-affiliated local group near you? Search on the NATRE website to find a local one, or ask NATRE for support to help set up a group yourself.

Curriculum planning

Part 2

Picking an RE curriculum

'Without a National Curriculum, I wondered what I was actually supposed to teach!'

Deciding what to teach in RE is key to ensuring you have good RE! However, how much freedom do RE teachers actually have to pick their own curriculum? Make sure you know what your school requires.

The teaching of RE is a legal requirement in schools in the UK, but the law does not explicitly state its content, unlike National Curriculum subjects.

Any local authority school needs to follow their LAS (locally agreed syllabus), as written by an ASC (Agreed Syllabus Conference), usually led by members of the SACRE (Standing Advisory Council on Religious Education).

A SACRE is a legal body created by the local authority, which will try to establish links with all schools in its area. The SACRE advises the local authority and supports the learning of RE. It is responsible for reviewing the LAS every five years.

Free schools and academies do not need to follow the LAS, but they need to have a syllabus that is in keeping with the law, reflecting the fact that religious traditions in Great Britain are, in the main, Christian (although this is now contested!) while taking into account other religions represented in the country. This is found in their funding agreement.

Voluntary-aided schools of a religious character, usually called 'faith schools', have RE provided in accordance with the school's trust deed, in accordance with the beliefs of the school. Voluntary-controlled schools of a religious character follow the LAS, unless parents request otherwise.

How many religions?

'It is worth thinking about what you consider a religiously literate student to be.'

RE in England remains, by law, predominantly Christian. At GCSE, it is now a requirement that students study two religions, one of which needs to be Christianity. However, you need to decide what students will study during Key Stage 3 (KS3).

Some schools will aim to cover the 'big six' in KS3 (Christianity, Judaism, Islam, Hinduism, Sikhism and Buddhism). Most schools also cover non-religious worldviews (such as Humanism) along with other disciplinary units, for example, 'What is a religion?'.

An average KS3 curriculum would give 120 hours: one hour a week, for 40 weeks, over three years. Allowing for a few missed lessons over the three years, to cover the big six and non-religious worldviews would mean around 15 or 16 lessons per religion. This is arguably enough time and allows for sufficient depth, but it does not make time for other disciplines and areas of interest to be covered.

Key questions to ask when planning your KS3 curriculum include:

- Who are your students and what is their faith background (and does this matter)?
- What does your curriculum model look like? (For example, is there an LAS you have to follow?)
- How much time do you have? How much time do you need?

> **Teaching tip**
>
> Studying in more depth can mean a reduction in breadth, and you will need to find the right balance and compromise between both.

Drop-down days

'With RE not being timetabled for Key Stage 5, we cover RE via drop-down days.'

If RE does not find a regular slot as a discrete subject, it can often be left to drop-down days. These can be fantastic as they give a whole day of curriculum time over to the subject, yet there is a lot of key organisation that needs to be done in advance.

Here are a few things to consider:

Teaching tip

Try to use speakers or organisations that you have worked with before and who are used to days like these. Once you get it right, you can do drop-down days year after year with great success!

- **Aims:** what are your aims? How will you follow up? How will you measure the usefulness and effectiveness of the day?
- **Timetable:** will it fit into the usual day? Will scheduled talks fit into lesson slots? If not, how will you manage this? How will movement around school be managed if not at usual changeover times?
- **Staffing:** this is linked to timetabling. If you are not keeping to the usual timings, will staff be walking in and out? Is it possible to have the same staff all day? How will you prepare them so they are not just sitting in the corner catching up on marking?
- **Visitors:** do they all know the key information – DBS, parking, school context, timetable for the day? Who will look after them all day and during breaks? Where will they have a cup of tea or go to the toilet?
- **Facilities:** what do speakers need for their presentations? What will you do if IT facilities fail or you get a surprise request on the day?

Some ideas you could consider for the day's theme are: theology of the body (relationships, equality, gender, disability, etc.); the environment (religious NGOs, ethics, stewardship, etc.); freedom (slavery, religious freedom, justice, etc.); evil and suffering (religious responses, natural/moral evil, etc.); and interfaith dialogue.

Non-religious worldviews

'Why would you study non-religious views in RE?'

Since 2015, it has been legally recognised that RE must cover both religious and non-religious worldviews. Students you teach may well be non-religious, and therefore a study of their beliefs or worldviews is inclusive for them.

Just because people aren't religious, or don't subscribe to an organised or recognised religion, does not mean they don't have beliefs and moral frameworks. Non-religious people describe themselves in a wide variety of ways, with many not fitting into a particular category or under a specific label. Their morality is often based on a social framework, built around the 'golden rule' (treat others as you want to be treated), which is a feature of most religions and which some claim predates any recognisable religious doctrine.

Key vocabulary

It's useful if students are familiar with key terms such as: agnostic, antitheist, atheist, humanist, rationalist, sceptic and secularist. As part of your study of non-religious worldviews you can ensure they understand the differences between these concepts, while realising that identity within them can be complex.

Taking it further

In the 2011 census, over a quarter of the UK identified as non-religious. The census is not the only source of such data; others include the British Social Attitudes survey and British Religion in Numbers. Students often enjoy interrogating and presenting data (a great classroom display).

Questions to ask include:

- Is the data reliable? (Check the source!)
- Should the data affect what we study in RE?
- What changes should happen in the UK given the data?
- What is the local data for my school?

Expanding boundaries

'I'm not even sure where the idea of the "big six" came from? It seems very limiting when considering the global religious and non-religious worldwide community.'

Christianity, Islam, Judaism, Hinduism, Sikhism and Buddhism: the staples of KS3 RE. While it's already a struggle to teach all of these well in three years, it's worth considering what else is missing. You may find that other world religions provide 'better' examples for the topic you are studying.

Teaching tip

Bear in mind that it is not a teacher's role to determine which groups are or aren't members of a faith, but to respect and recognise every group's right to self-identify as they wish. In other words, our job is to teach, not preach.

In *Beyond the Big Six Religions**, Dr James Holt explores a range of diversity often not covered in RE such as:

- **Christianity:** The Church of Jesus Christ of Latter-day Saints and Jehovah's Witnesses.
- **Islam:** Shi'a and Ahmadiyya Islam.
- **Other:** Bahá'í, Humanism, Jainism, Paganism, Rastafari.

As always, there is the challenge of how to include more: *if I do this, what do I not do?* Below are some ideas for how to include more diversity in your teaching.

Recognising diversity

There are a few things that 'all Christians do...' or 'all Muslims believe...' – but not many! Ensure the language you model in the classroom recognises this. You can highlight some of the different views on certain topics as you explain key ideas. This creates a basic awareness of the fact there is more to be learned!

Teaching diversity

*Holt, J (2019), *Beyond the Big Six Religions: Expanding the Boundaries in the Teaching of Religion and Worldviews.* Chester: University of Chester Press.

In an approach to RE that explores themes and topics, it's possible to include religions that have expression in the local community. For example, when exploring Christian baptism, or initiation rites in different religions, it's possible to look at various other groups, whether this is baptism within the Church of Jesus Christ of Latter-day Saints at the age of eight, or the spiritual process and declaration of becoming a Bahá'í.

Another example could be exploring the topic of religious environmentalism. Both Jainism and manifestations of Paganism can be seen to be far more 'connected' and 'environmentally friendly' than some expressions of the big six.

At Key Stage 4 (KS4) and Key Stage 5 (KS5), there are specific topics that lend themselves more to some of the issues within smaller religions. For example, exploring the motivations behind the establishment of Rastafari can be an example of a Marxist interpretation of society, and the need to rebel or find a voice in a structure that does not recognise the voice of the minority.

'Beyond the big six' unit/project

While you may not be able to devote lesson time to all the different faiths and beliefs listed above, some teachers have had success with a unit or project that covers the basics of a number of these. One idea is to give students a faith or group each, then research this and share back with the class. (However, be aware that Dr James Holt suggests this can lead to tokenism and weaving them throughout the curriculum is potentially far more beneficial to students and their understanding of the beliefs.)

Display

Create a wall display featuring some of the above faiths and beliefs. It could rotate through these, or cover a couple of them in reasonable detail. Do you have a group of students who could work on this?

Drop-down day

If you have drop-down days in RE, consider devoting a day to faiths other than the big six.

Taking it further

Look at your local area to identity any places of worship that are not covered by your curriculum. This is an argument given by supporters of local determination for RE – students need to understand their local area.

Not RE

'When our time is limited, I find it useful to review my schemes of work and individual lessons to look at what is *not* RE and try to cut out or cut down these activities.'

If more time is spent on something that isn't directly RE, is it worth it?

In an attempt to get a 'hook' or find a way into a topic, we can all add something to our lesson which at best is a minor distraction and at worst is lost learning time. This is a form of the argument that 'religion is everywhere' and therefore anything goes in the RE curriculum. Using 'hooks' can be useful, as long as you make sure that there is a clear link with RE and don't lose too much learning time. Consider these three examples:

Example 1: What are the effects of having to fast during Ramadan for premiership footballers? What religious knowledge is needed? Muslims fast during Ramadan. What biology- or PE-related knowledge is needed? Lots!

Example 2: Create a newspaper front page of the story of Ganesha. What takes longer: to explain the story of Ganesha or to explain how to set out a newspaper front page (headline, columns, quotes, tense, reporting styles, etc.)?

Example 3: Produce a tourist brochure for the Golden Temple. This requires images, maps, directions, flight routes, architectural features, the political history of Amritsar...

So how do you ensure the RE in each of these examples?

Example 1: Why do premiership footballers see it as important to fast during Ramadan? Focus on the universal challenges of fasting and reasons for fasting.

Example 2: Liaise with the English department. What techniques have students learnt recently in English language that you could use in RE? If they have just learnt about newspaper front pages, it may be a great idea!

Example 3: Structure the brochure with a framework. Plan out exactly what students do or don't need to include (add labelled boxes, for example).

I've found that I have rejected ideas as the non-RE knowledge and explanation was too time-consuming to justify the 'hook'.

Taking it further

Students can get good at spotting when something is really a religious issue. Challenge them to consider whether an issue is religious or perhaps political, cultural, historical or geographical?

Scripting in RE

'Scripted lessons have seen a resurgence, but does it remove the need for the teacher?'

There are many different ways in which lessons can be considered to include 'scripted' elements. Here are three ways that RE could be improved by the use of scripts; they may be particularly useful for non-specialists.

Scripted explanations: Some ideas in RE are very complex. An idea such as Real Presence in the Eucharist for Catholics can prove challenging even for experienced RE teachers. To prepare a short script, which carefully and accurately explains the concept, can be hugely beneficial to teachers. It also ensures the teacher has clarified their own subject knowledge before standing in front of a class to articulate it.

Scripted sequencing: There are some things which need a really clear order and structure to them. This may not be obvious to the non-specialist or even the new RE teacher. For example, to understand the synagogue in Judaism, it would make sense to have looked at the Tabernacle in the wilderness and the Temples in Jerusalem first.

Scripted questioning: Questioning is a real skill and one that teachers develop over time. There can be real value in writing out questions in advance and even allocating them to certain students. Deviation will naturally happen, but scripting should ensure that the key points you want to address are covered. It can also limit the time given to class discussion to aid with time management.

Scripts can easily be shared across the department, ensuring that different areas of strength and expertise are utilised.

Raising the
profile of RE

Part 3

Host a philosophy evening

'It was one of the moments that you get every now and then in your career, that makes your job really worthwhile and leaves you buzzing for months.' (*Claire Doherty*)

Give your students an opportunity to showcase their work to their school and their parents.

This fantastic idea from Claire Doherty was inspired by Ron Berger's book *An Ethic of Excellence** as a way of allowing students to prepare for a public evening where they really need to know their stuff! It's also a great way of getting parents involved, helping them to realise what their child is doing and the value of the subject.

Preparation

Students work individually or in small groups to prepare presentations on an aspect of the course. They need to be experts as they will be taking questions from the audience! Students also design their own invitations and publicity for the event and manage the guest list.

The evening

The students take turns presenting their key concepts or ideas. There are questions to and from the audience, with students managing the discussion.

An interval can provide an opportunity for refreshments (managed by the students themselves), giving guests time to look at displays created by the students.

*Berger, R (2003), *An Ethic of Excellence: Building a Culture of Craftsmanship with Students*. Portsmouth, NH: Heinemann.

The second half concludes the presentations, after which there could be further discussion and debate, and a quiz to finish. There might be an award for the best presentation.

Get an REQM (RE Quality Mark)

'This really lifted the profile of RE in the school. My senior leadership team realised we were doing a fantastic job as a department.'

This can really raise the profile of the subject within school and enable the department to showcase its good work. It can help the department team to feel recognised and valued externally, and can also help to drive improvement.

The REQM (RE Quality Mark) was set up by The Religious Education Council of England and Wales to recognise outstanding learning and teaching in religious education. It has three levels of award: Gold, Silver and Bronze. There is a charge to apply, which covers the assessor's visit. (There are grants for small schools and those in Ofsted categories 3 and 4 to cover some of the cost.)

The award is focused around enhanced pedagogy, so the accreditation system is designed to show how RE contributes to whole-school improvement.

After filling in an application form, you will need to start to collect both school and learner evidence; the process shouldn't take more than a day's worth of time in total. There are often nearby schools who are willing to help and advise which level of award to apply for.

The five key areas that evidence is needed for are: learners and learning; teachers and teaching; the curriculum; subject leadership; and continuing professional development.

> **Teaching tip**
>
> Don't do this as a one off! The REQM can provide a useful tool for self-evaluation within the department. How do you work towards Gold? How can you maintain and go beyond the Gold award?

The RE trip

'Our trip to New York really put the department on the map! Students were talking about it for months, years even!'

A visit to a place of worship can make a great day or even half-day out, but you could really get the excitement about RE going with a trip abroad! This may take several years of planning and parental payments, but the value for students and the wider school community can be huge.

Here are a few ideas – in approximate order of distance from the UK – with a few suggested itinerary stop-offs:

- **Amsterdam:** Anne Frank's house and other sites connected to Jewish persecution, Our Lord in the Attic Church, Westermoskee (mosque).
- **Rome:** St Peter's Basilica, the Coliseum, the Catacombs, the Pantheon, the Mosque of Rome, the Great Synagogue of Rome.
- **Israel:** Jerusalem including the Haram al-Sharif/Temple Mount, Nazareth, Bethlehem, the Sea of Galilee.
- **New York:** the United Nations, the Harlem Civil Rights Walking Tour, the 9/11 Memorial, St Patrick's Cathedral, the Jewish Museum.
- **India:** the Golden Temple in Amritsar, Dharamsala (home of the Dalai Lama), the Taj Mahal.

Competitions

'It's cross-curricular, it's high profile... and the students love taking part! Every student enters.'

Entering your students for competitions can have a variety of benefits. It gives them external motivation, plus an audience for their work. Sometimes it's as simple as the prizes! It's another way to raise the profile of the department within the school. University-based competitions may have some prestige and be useful for UCAS statements.

Art competitions

NATRE's Spirited Arts competition began in 2004, and around 20,000 students take part each year. They are not just from the UK and entries come from all over the world. Many schools incorporate the competition into their RE lessons via a 'Spirited Arts' unit of work or as a specialist RE/arts week. It runs all year, and judging takes place in August. Each year there is a new theme, which is advertised via NATRE.

Essay competitions

Look out for these, particularly for A level students. They are often run by universities and Religious Studies faculties, as well as Oxbridge colleges. For example, St Mary's, Chester, St Andrew's, Trinity College (Cambridge) and Keble College (Oxford) have run some over the past few years. Some religious orders run them too. Prizes often involve book tokens or cash.

In-house competitions

The RE department could always launch its own competition! The department could set a title and arrange a prize, perhaps in conjunction with their local university. A local business may even help provide a prize.

Teaching tip

It's worth dedicating lesson time to introduce a competition. You may want it to be largely independent so students complete the task at home. However, simply presenting students with a flyer for a competition – unless there is a big cash prize – is unlikely to be successful!

Open evenings

'Most parents still do not know what modern RE is.'

Sadly, it's fairly typical for RE teachers to be told by prospective parents that it was a subject they disliked, or that it's just an opinions- or discussion-based subject. Give parents and students a different impression at open evenings.

The RE classroom can often be one of the most popular locations on the school tour, as RE teachers are used to having to sell their subject and do it well. Here are some ideas:

- **Students:** students who love RE will demonstrate how brilliant the subject is without you having to do a thing!
- **Experiential experience:** in some schools you could try having candles, incense or music – this can signify that something a little different happens in RE. It can create a feeling of calm, which is perhaps the opposite to departments trying to impress with bangs and flashes!
- **Philosophy and ethics:** big questions and ethical dilemmas can provide interesting talking points for prospective students. For example, you could use the 'trolley problem' – a well-known thought experiment. Would you kill one person to save five people?
- **Online quizzes:** if you have computers or laptops, setting up some model quizzes (such as ones that you use for homework) can show the demands of the subject.
- **Food:** it is perfectly reasonable to have food and sometimes, the seemingly tenuous links can be good conversation starters (why are halal or kosher sweets important?).
- **Work:** get those best books out!
- **Results:** having a few posters around the room with GCSE and A level results is ideal.

Abrahamic faiths

Part 4

How to teach the Eucharist (Christianity)

'Surely it can't be the actual body of Christ?'

The important thing is to communicate the teachings accurately! There is some deep thinking to be done here too: why do different Christian churches believe different things? Can Christians receive the bread in different denominational churches?

Teaching tip

Exploring the idea of 'mystery' in both an everyday and religious sense before covering a topic like this can help students to realise they might not fully understand it!

Taking it further

To understand Catholic beliefs of transubstantiation, a basic understanding of Aristotelian metaphysics as put forward by Thomas Aquinas can stretch the most able students – the *substance* changes, without the *species* (appearance) changing.

The following information could be organised and used in a lesson in a variety of ways. You could ask students to put the information into a table to highlight similarities and differences.

- Catholics believe that the bread and wine are transformed into the actual body and blood of Christ; this is called the Real Presence. Transubstantiation is one explanation of this mystery. The Mass is a 'making present' of the Last Supper, with the priest *in persona Christi* (in the person of Christ).
- Orthodox Christians also believe a real change takes place, but they do not see the need to explain it.
- Anglican views vary, with different interpretations of the presence of Jesus in the Eucharist. Generally, and officially, they believe in the real presence of 'objective reality', but this is interpreted differently: for example, some would see it as a 'pneumatic presence', which is a spiritual presence.
- Anabaptists, Latter-day Saints and Jehovah's Witnesses are examples of **memorialism**, where Jesus is only present in the hearts and minds of believers.
- Quakers and the Salvation Army are examples of **suspension**, where there are no links to the Last Supper (that is, no bread) in services.

How to teach the Resurrection (Christianity)

'If Jesus has not been raised, then our faith is worthless; and we are to be pitied above all men.' (*1 Corinthians 15:14*)

Perhaps the greatest mystery of them all: did Jesus really rise from the dead? Or was it a hoax? This can be a great hook into a lesson on the Resurrection.

Investigating this key event can help students to understand its place at the centre of Christianity. Start by comparing narratives of the Resurrection from the Bible: what is in all four accounts? This forms the backbone of your evidence. Investigate each possible theory below (and there are many more!). We can't go back and do a full modern-day crime-scene investigation, so we have to use the evidence we have...

Apparent death theory: Jesus wasn't really dead and had only fainted. But weren't the Romans highly effective at execution? Didn't Jesus suffer extensive injuries before and during the crucifixion?

Theft theory: Jesus's body was stolen. But would thieves overpower the Roman guards? Would the disciples have been transformed in their outlook if the resurrection hadn't actually happened? Wouldn't people have displayed the stolen body to discredit early Christianity?

Hallucination theory: Jesus was seen after his death due to hallucinations. But would all witnesses have had the same hallucination? Would it have lasted for 40 days?

With students as investigators, they need to assess the evidence and draw conclusions. Based on the evidence, is it more or less likely that the Resurrection took place?

> **Teaching tip**
>
> This can be set up as a full investigation for the students. You could give some of the students different pieces of evidence, and others a possible theory. They then have to discuss and compare the evidence to draw their own conclusions.

> **Bonus idea** ★
>
> Get students to compare an extract from Chapter 15 of *The Lion, The Witch and The Wardrobe* and draw parallels to the crucifixion and resurrection narratives in the Bible. To what extent is C. S. Lewis presenting Aslan as being like Jesus?

How to teach the Trinity (Christianity)

'Three does not mean three, one does not mean one, and person does not mean person.' (*Bishop David Jenkins*)

There are many ways in which you can help your students to understand the key beliefs and relationships in the Trinity.

Teaching tip

A discussion of the types of heresy (beliefs contrary to orthodox doctrine) should lead students to be good critics of the bad analogies.

The Trinity is a topic that teachers have frequently found a challenge to explain to students. Many Christians will refer to it as a 'Mystery' – as something that cannot be fully explained. The early Church ruled out many explanations that were considered to be heresy, yet these often continue in the RE classroom today!

Bad analogies

Using bad analogies is a great way to teach what the Trinity is not. Why do they not quite explain the Trinity?

- **White–yolk–shell (egg):** this is compositionalism (made up of different parts).
- **Ice–water–steam:** this is modalism (one God with different modes or 'faces').
- **Three-leaf clover:** this is compositionalism (despite its alleged use by St Patrick in Ireland).
- **Cake–jam–chocolate (jaffa cake):** this is compositionalism.
- **Dad–husband–teacher:** this is modalism.
- **Father–Son–Grandson:** this is subordinationism (a hierarchy where one is subordinate to the others).
- **A family:** this is tritheism (three distinct gods).

A useful diagram

This diagram depicts the relationships in the Trinity.

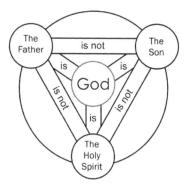

Rearranging the story

Early Christians did not start with the Mystery of the Trinity and then work backwards like we often try to do in the classroom. They believed that God was one (Deuteronomy 6:4–9), they believed that Jesus was the true Son of God (Philippians 2:5–11), and they believed the Spirit was God (Romans 8:26 and Galatians 4:6). This led them to believe God was one (ousios), but distinctly three (hypostasis), equal (homoousios) and in a circular and dynamic relationship (perichoresis) – the result was the Trinity!

Using art

Pick some artwork depicting the Trinity and ask your students questions about it. Does this piece show oneness? Distinctiveness? Equality? Dynamism? How does it draw in the observer?

Examples you could pick include Rublev's *The Trinity*, William Blake's Trinity sketch, Cósida's *The Holy Trinity* and Masaccio's *The Holy Trinity*.

Teaching tip

1 + 1 + 1 = 3, but 1 x 1 x 1 = 1. How does this relate to the Trinity?

Taking it further

Investigate the early councils of the Church and their impact on the teaching of the Trinity. For example, the First Council of Nicea (325) focused on Jesus being one with God, while the First Council of Constantinople (381) ensured that the Holy Spirit was seen as one with God and Jesus. Start by reading the different versions of the Creed and looking at references to the Trinity in each.

Teaching about the prophets (Islam)

'Should I add PBUH when I am teaching about Muhammad?'

It is important to discuss and explain the abbreviations PBUH and SAWS and explain why most Muslims refrain from any images of the Prophet.

Naming Muhammad

Even if you don't use the abbreviations PBUH and SAWS, it's worth discussing and explaining to students why Muslims use these abbreviations.

When writing the name of the Prophet Muhammad, Muslims often follow it with the abbreviation 'PBUH' ('peace be upon him'). They will often say the full phrase when speaking. It is a response to this instruction in the Qur'an: 'Allah and His angels send blessings upon the Prophet. Oh you who believe! Send blessings upon him, and salute him with all respect' (Surah 33:56). But Muslims do not take offence when a non-Muslim simply refers to the Prophet as 'Muhammad'.

It is also useful to look at the variations such as 'SAWS'. These letters stand for the Arabic words *sallallahu alayhi wa sallam* ('may God's blessings and peace be with him').

When the names of other prophets or angels are mentioned, Muslims also wish peace upon them as well, using the phrase *alayhi salaam* ('peace be upon him'). This is sometimes abbreviated to 'AS'.

Depictions of Muhammad

Oral and written descriptions of the life of Muhammad are accepted by Muslims, but the visual depictions remain controversial.

Despite some early Islamic artwork portraying the Prophet, due to a number of hadiths, most Muslims now refrain from any images of the Prophet out of respect, and to avoid potentially committing shirk (associating partners with Allah).

Calligraphy forms the most common depiction of the Prophet in Islamic countries and communities. Various monograms and ambigrams of his name can be found online, including a wide variety of artistic forms such as mosaics, pottery and architecture.

Taking it further

Older students may be able to sensitively research the controversy around images of the Prophet Muhammad in recent times. See, for example, cartoons in the magazines *Jyllands-Posten* and *Charlie Hebdo*.

What is God like? (Islam)

'Artwork can provide a fantastic way into understanding Allah.'

Look at religious artwork with your students and consider encouraging students to create their own artwork.

Consider if it is a good use of time for students to create their own artwork. Is this helping understanding of Islam, or is it developing art or maths skills? Cross-curricular learning can be useful, but why not speak to other departments and see if they want to tie their lessons with yours?

Taking it further

Investigate the Mubarak Mosque in Tilford, Surrey (search online; there are some good videos on YouTube), which has a focus on the names of Allah.

Muslim tradition prohibits any attempt to depict Allah, as He is not a physical entity. The Qur'an states 'There is nothing like Him' (Surah 42:11) and 'No vision can take Him in' (Surah 6:103); therefore Muslims will try to understand His nature in other ways.

There is a huge range of Islamic artwork, but the most useful for teaching tend to be those connected with calligraphy, architecture and what is called 'arabesque'. These are geometrical floral or plant-like designs. They are used, often in mosque design, to symbolise the transcendent, indivisible and infinite nature of Allah. Ask students how they think the art depicts this. A hadith of the Prophet Muhammad says, 'Allah is beautiful and He loves beauty' (al-Mu'jam al-Awsat 6902) – do students think the artwork is beautiful?

The 99 names or attributes of Allah (such as 'Gracious', 'Merciful' and 'Master') have often been incorporated into artwork, in particular calligraphy. Just using a simple online image search can provide many examples. You can get students to collect a selection and use them to explore Allah's characteristics.

Unlike much other religious artwork (compare the wide and diverse variety in Christianity, for example), there are common features in all Islamic art. This provides a remarkable coherence. Students could easily identify some common themes from a collection of images: no human depictions, symmetry, similar shapes (leaves or flowers) and calligraphy.

What matters most? (Islam)

'Identifying what matters to a religious believer is the first step; what matters most is even more important to understand!'

Students could work in groups to arrange concepts, justifying their positions to their peers and then via class feedback.

As students get to grips with a religion, they will identify various beliefs, teachings and practices. It is important to try to contextualise and rationalise these. Here is a list of some key religious beliefs in Islam from Claire Clinton, an RE adviser:

The city of Mecca; the Qur'an; wudu washing for prayer; stories of the Prophet; obeying parents; daily prayer; learning Arabic; believing in angels; the mosque; Friday prayers; a clean prayer mat; celebrating Eid Al Fitr; paradise; doing Zakat; wearing traditional clothes; being generous with money; fasting in Ramadan; becoming Hajji; the call to prayer; doing what Allah commands.

Invite students to arrange these concepts, working in groups, before justifying their decisions to their peers. There are various different ways these can then be arranged, but a simple hierarchy is unlikely to work! For example, a diagram with concentric circles (like a dartboard) could be a useful tool. It may be useful to give students labels for these circles such as 'crucial', 'important', 'less important' and 'not important'.

Teaching tip

This could be a worthwhile task before attempting an evaluation question or a longer essay. Think carefully about what concepts you want to include!

Celebrating festivals (Judaism)

'Shabbat is a weekly reminder and celebration of the covenant between The Almighty and the Jewish people.'

Ask your students to research a Jewish festival and then write an invitation to a festival celebration.

Taking it further

Invitations can work well with any religion. A similar idea is to create a simple guide for a place of worship. What will you see and hear, and why? How should you dress and behave?

Rosh Hashanah, Yom Kippur, Sukkot, Passover and Shavuot are viewed as the most important festivals in Judaism and require a time of rest from work. However, Shabbat also demands this, hence some class it as a festival too.

Compare and contrast

Research Jewish festivals with the students, looking at key aspects such as:

- Timing (dates; how long it lasts for).
- Historical meaning (what is being remembered and why).
- Focus (the main theme of the festival).
- Practice (what Jewish people do during the festival).
- Food (what Jewish people eat or avoid).

Invitations

Ask students to write an invitation to a non-Jew for the celebration of a Jewish festival. This can enable them to articulate what will happen and why. The context of it being celebrated with family in the home means that a guest would benefit from being briefed. For example, as well as explaining what will happen, the invitation could explain whether the guest should bring anything or wear anything special.

Bonus idea ★

A lesson can be livened up with some great contemporary Jewish music. Check out The Maccabeats (*Candlelight* or *Purim Song*) or Six13 (*Uptown Passover* or *Chanukah*).

Dharmic faiths

Part 5

Mindfulness (Buddhism)

'Investigating mindfulness brought a calm in my classroom –
it helped students focus and really think about the practice and
its uses.'

**Mindfulness is central to understanding the Noble Eightfold Path
in Buddhism. Try introducing students to the idea of mindfulness
through the activity of eating. These ideas were suggested by Neil
McKain, Head of Religious Studies.**

Teaching tip

Be aware that some
students may not
be comfortable with
mindfulness due to
its roots in religious
tradition. Mindfulness
may be promoted as a
purely secular activity,
yet it is clearly a Buddhist
practice. It may be that
some students will not
wish to take part and
their wishes should be
respected.

Taking it further

Allow students to
consider other practices
that could be done
mindfully, such as
mindful seeing (taking
in every small detail
from a window view)
or mindful listening
(practising engaged and
active listening). A good
question to ask students
is: does being mindful
help people to live a
better life?

People do many things without much
awareness of what they are doing. A good
example is eating: do we eat mindfully? Ask
students:

- Do we consider what we are eating?
- Do we consider who has worked and
  suffered to provide us with the food?
- Do we focus on the taste and texture of
  the food, or do we simply shovel it into our
  mouths?

In Zen Buddhism, mindful eating is a common
practice. It can be attempted with a simple
classroom activity. Pick a small food item, such
as a slice of apple, a grape or a chocolate or
sweet.

- Firstly, get students to carefully observe the
  item, thinking about its colour, shape and
  texture.
- Students then put it in their mouth, chewing
  slowly and carefully, focusing on its taste.
- As the food is swallowed, they should think
  of the people who have grown and produced
  the item. Is there something to be grateful
  for?

Students then write up a short reflection of the
experience, linking this clearly to the Noble
Eightfold Path ('how does mindful eating help
Buddhists to follow the Noble Eightfold Path?').

Impermanence (Buddhism)

'My students really struggled with the idea of impermanence as one of the three marks of existence in Buddhism.'

For Buddhists, all things are in a constant state of flux; everything physical and mental begins and then ends. For students to fully understand this concept, they may need some assistance and examples.

Using photos

Look at photos taken over time of a famous team, such as three different photos of the England football team:

- What differences do you see in the photos? (Different players or kits, for example.)
- What has changed over time? (Different hair styles or kit designs, for example.)
- What has stayed the same? (The three lions crest or the number of players, for example.)

Nothing lasts

I always use a sped-up film of a flower or fruit bowl rotting to illustrate impermanence. It's a good image to use with students as Buddhists offer cut flowers at temples as a visual reminder of impermanence.

The key idea for students to comprehend is that nothing actually lasts that long; although football teams may feel like 'permanent' things, they change over time, and at school the student body and staff change year on year. For Buddhists, human life embodies this cycle of repeated birth and death (samsara).

This then leads to an understanding of anatta: the idea of there being no unchanging, permanent self or soul. When enlightenment is reached, this is a state of realisation about this lack of self.

Taking it further

Staff photos from your school could be used to show a gradual flux of staff turnover. Each year, some stay and some go... If the photos are available, how far back do you have to go to find no current staff?

The four sights (Buddhism)

'Students enjoy relating their studies to real life.'

Invite students to make connections between the four sights and recent stories they have heard in the news.

The four sights are four events described in the accounts of Gautama Buddha's life. He had led a sheltered life until this point, not experiencing any of these things. The four sights led to him rejecting his royal family and embarking on a journey to find the answer to suffering.

Students could research recent news stories that would 'shock' in today's world, linked to the first three sights. For example:

- **The old man:** what does it mean to be old? What difficulties do the elderly face in today's world?
- **The sick man:** what does it mean to be sick or healthy? What issues do we face with health in today's world?
- **The dead man:** what does death mean? Why does it cause great sadness? What are the leading causes of death in today's world?

The fourth sight the Buddha saw was a wise man (an ascetic). The Buddha was impressed with the sense of peace coming from the wise man and this inspired him to try following asceticism himself. What might be the equivalent of the fourth sight in today's world for students? For example, a religious leader or a charity? What action might today's 'four sights' prompt students to take? They are unlikely to become an ascetic themselves... but perhaps they might do more charitable acts?

Hukamnama (Sikhism)

'How can students understand the nature of the Guru Granth Sahib?'

Help students to understand that the Guru Granth Sahib is much more than just a 15th-century piece of literature.

To a non-Sikh, the Guru Granth Sahib may seem to be just a book. But to a Sikh, the Guru Granth Sahib is their living, breathing, talking spiritual guide or guru.

Every day in the early hours of the morning, the Guru Granth Sahib is opened and a hymn, chosen at random, called a Hukamnama, is issued from the Harmandir Sahib in Amritsar. It is shared online, via email, smartphone apps and so on, and is then displayed in the foyer of each gurdwara.

- Get students to find out what the Hukamnama for the day is.
- Study it carefully to work out what kind of questions the quote could answer.
- What might Sikhs learn or understand from it?
- How might a Sikh try to put it into action that day?

The living, breathing, talking spiritual guide or guru

Sikhs see the Guru Granth Sahib as far more than a book. Showing students images of how the book is kept and looked after can help them to understand its status, for example, images of it on the *takht* (throne), being fanned by the *chaur sahib*, and being put to bed.

Taking it further

Understanding the need for a guru today is important. Evaluate the advantages and challenges of the Guru Granth Sahib being seen as a living guru.

Polytheism or monotheism? (Hinduism)

'How do I explain to my students that Hinduism doesn't really fit into usual definitions?'

It's usual to find 'monotheism' and 'polytheism' in the key-word lists of most RE departments. However, this can become very problematic when studying Hinduism as the definitions don't fit what Hindus believe!

Although there are many different Hindu gods or deities, Hindus believe that all these deities are manifestations of one divine entity who is known as Brahman. In simple terms, Hindus believe that if they worship Brahman through a form they understand, or which has meaning to them, they will find it easier to worship.

My favourite approach is to look at common misconceptions about Hinduism and break down why each of these are potentially incorrect. This can help students to understand the complexities of Hindu belief. For example:

- There are 330 million Hindu gods.
- Hindus are idol worshipers.
- Cows are holy.
- All Hindus are vegetarians.
- The Bhagavad Gita is the holy book.

Having explored these misconceptions, and after studying some of the different gods (particularly the Trimurti), it can be worthwhile looking at some other ways of understanding Hindu belief:

- **Monistic:** believing in a 'oneness' of the universe.
- **Henotheistic:** worship of one God, without ruling out other gods.

Puja (Hinduism)

'Can you make sense of this?'

Puja involves all five senses. It's the form of Hindu worship that ranges from brief daily rites in the home to elaborate temple rituals. Allowing students to experience something of a puja ceremony can really help to bring the study of Hinduism alive.

One option is simply to watch a video. However, even with this option, you can help students by using other senses. Showing images of water, a bell, a flame, incense, flowers, offerings (fruit, rice or milk) and kumkuma powders can help make it memorable and allow students to consider the meaning and inference of these objects.

These could be provided in a card-sort or pairs exercise, where students have to match the item with its meaning:

- **Flame:** divine light and wisdom.
- **Incense:** loving presence.
- **Flowers:** beauty and purity.
- **Food stuffs:** offering to the gods.
- **Bells:** recreate the sound of Aum.
- **Kumkuma:** used to create a 'third eye' to allow sight of the divine.

Studying puja chants can also give an insight into the characteristics of the different gods. For example:

- 'Om gam ganapataye namaha': 'I bow to the elephant-faced deity who is capable of removing all obstacles. I pray for blessings and protection' (Ganesh).
- 'Om shrim maha lakshmiyei swaha': 'Om and salutations to she who manifests every kind of abundance' (Lakshmi).

Teaching tip

Students will appreciate seeing different types of puja, and videos or images can help them to understand the variety of worship. Get them to identify differences and similarities.

Complex or controversial topics

Part 6

Extremism and fundamentalism

'Students struggle to distinguish between these terms, and they are often used interchangeably in the media.'

A simple table can help students to unpick the subtle differences between extremism and fundamentalism.

Teaching tip

TrueTube has a good video on Muslim extremism and fundamentalism at https://www.truetube.co.uk/film/extremists.

Nearly all religions have at least some form of fundamentalism or extremism. It is useful to define the two terms:

- **Extremism** can be defined as both misuse of religion with violent intentions, and a form of extreme conservatism, wanting others to follow your own religion.
- **Fundamentalism** is the meticulous and strict adherence to a set of beliefs, often wanting to return to an earlier time in the religion.

Ask students to make a table highlighting the differences between the two terms. An analogy can be helpful too:

- Person A loves their football team, but does not like the fact some people watch their team on TV, but also enjoy watching other teams on the TV.
- Person B loves football, particularly when it gives them an excuse to meet up with some mates and have a fight with fans of the opposing team.
- Person C wants everyone to support their team, and on match days will shout at opposition fans in the stadium.

If football was a religion: person A = fundamentalist, person B = violent extremist, and person C = non-violent extremist.

Bonus idea ★

Why not use Gandhi as an example to research? He was clearly a fundamentalist but followed the principle of *ahimsa* (non-violence). Students could research examples of his fundamentalist beliefs, as well as his rejections of extremism.

Dealing with death

'RE tackles many of the tough issues, and RE teachers naturally become skilled in dealing with them well.'

Death will feature on your curriculum at various points, perhaps linked to funerals and other death rituals, beliefs about life after death, or the deaths of people like Jesus or Martin Luther King. It is not something to be approached flippantly, and needs to be done well.

Preparation

- Ask pastoral staff about any issues concerning bereavement.
- If there is an issue, a quiet word from either yourself or pastoral staff about what is coming up is important. It may be that you need to delay the topic, or excuse the student.
- Alert the whole class that it's coming up. Don't do it in such a way to create hysteria, but to give students a chance to see you or another member of staff in advance.

The lesson

- Remind students that this is a difficult topic for some to discuss and that they don't know what everyone has been through.
- Use clear vocabulary so students know exactly what you are talking about. 'He's crossed over' or 'she's asleep' may mean something to adults but not young people.
- Give students time to think things through; it will often raise difficult questions for them.
- Admit that you don't know everything.

After the lesson

- Remind pastoral staff that this topic has been discussed.
- Check written work carefully to see if students have written anything that needs following up.

> **Teaching tip**
>
> Get the balance right! You don't want the lesson to be jokey and light-hearted, but you don't want it to be too morose and morbid. Judge your class and their mood. It's important to get the timing and context of lessons right.

Masculinity in RE

'RE gives some amazing opportunities to discuss and critique masculinity.' (*Matt Pinkett*)

It's claimed that traditional ideas about masculinity are having a detrimental effect on boys (and indeed girls) in school. RE provides a great opportunity to discuss and evaluate these problems.

Discussions around masculinity could easily feature in lessons looking specifically at gender roles, a topic that often features on GCSE specifications. However, there are some really interesting opportunities to explore issues of masculinity in other areas too. Here are three examples.

Non-violence

'Put your sword back in its place,' Jesus said to him. 'All who take the sword will die by the sword.' (Matthew 26:52)

- Do men and women respond differently to someone who is about to be wrongly detained?
- Would some men have been impressed by one of Jesus's followers cutting off the high priest's servant's ear? Why?

'An eye for an eye only ends up making the whole world blind.' (Mahatma Gandhi)

- Even Gandhi's followers found his non-violence frustrating at times. Why do you think they found it so frustrating? Do you think men or women probably found it the most frustrating? Why?

Celibacy

Buddhist monks, most Hindu monks and Catholic priests all practise celibacy. Jewish rabbis are encouraged to have big families, as are Muslim Imams.

- Is fertility seen as a measure of masculinity?
- Is a man who freely chooses to abstain from sexual activity in some way 'less of a man'?

Charitable giving

Charitable giving is an important feature in all major religions, from Zakat in Islam to Dāna in Buddhism.

- Is it harder to be charitable if you are a man? Why?
- Is there a difference between giving money and giving time?
- Are men more likely to give money than time?
- Do men feel that doing big, public gestures impresses people?

Taking it further

Further reading: *Boys Don't Try: Rethinking Masculinity in Schools* by Matt Pinkett and Mark Roberts (Routledge, 2019).

Introducing biblical hermeneutics

'If "context is king", what does this mean for the Bible?'

Introducing a hermeneutical approach can make the study of any part of scripture far more engaging and interesting in the RE classroom. It showcases the multiple layers of meaning that are discernable in texts. It can encourage students to think about how people discern and search for meaning and allows them to become participants in that process.

Teaching tip

Try showing how quoting out of context can be dangerous! 'It's a great book, if you don't need a plot or character development' in a review could easily be quoted as 'It's a great book' on the front cover. A text without a context is just a pretext.

Biblical hermeneutics is the study of the interpretation of the Bible. Exploring hermeneutics can change the way students approach the study of the text, for example, they can link together theological, philosophical, historical, cultural and sociological questions and responses. It can help build bridges between different interpretations, giving a further depth of understanding.

Are all texts within the Bible the same, or can we learn things from knowing that a quote is from a letter or a psalm, a gospel or a history? Investigating the author is also important. For example, Mark wrote for persecuted Christians in Rome, Luke wrote to the Gentiles, while Matthew wrote to Jews who had converted. This may explain differences in the nativity story and give insight into how the text was heard or read by the first hearers or readers.

It is vital to provide students with historical, cultural and geographical information relevant to the text. This gives the context of the time and the place. For example, what was Corinth like at the time of St Paul's writing? How does this help us understand the letters to the early Church?

There are also translation issues with the Bible texts we use. For example, does Judas 'hand over' or 'betray' Jesus, and does it matter? GCSE RS can discourage the study of text within a context, with students just looking at individual phrases. For example, in 1 Corinthians 14:34, Paul says 'women should be kept silent in the churches', which is often quoted negatively. Yet a little earlier, Paul had spoken positively about women praying and prophesising. Teaching students to find meaning by drawing on a range of texts, rather than just one or two quotes, is an introduction to the traditional way the Bible is interpreted.

Meaning is something that happens in the mind of the reader through their own experience and perception. Encouraging students to read the text through a different perspective can also help them to understand how it can be interpreted in different ways. For example, we often look at parables as examples of allegory and models of right behaviour. However, this is an oversimplification and they don't all work in the same way. 'The Good Samaritan' is not just about helping a stranger! It is about the fact that people in positions of Jewish authority ignored the man in need, and it was the Samaritan (considered unpure as of mixed Jewish and Gentile heritage) who did stop and help.

You could also mention how women or mothers might have particular insights into passages about motherhood, birth and the death of children.

Taking it further

In a bigger sense, hermeneutics applies to all perceptions of reality, not just the Bible and not just sacred texts. How people are moved or touched by sacred art, for example, is also a process of hermeneutics. How people interpret a point of view in a debate is also a process of hermeneutics. It is a tool of critical thinking that can empower the student beyond the confines of RE.

Introducing utilitarianism

'The greatest good for the greatest number can be oversimplified by students; they need to understand the complexities of pleasure!'

Making a topic relevant to students needs to be done carefully. How can you provide genuine insight, without a tenuous link or dumbing down the topic too much? A. J. Smith, an RE teacher, suggested this brilliant way of teaching John Stuart Mill's higher and lower pleasures.

Taking it further

Don't forget Jeremy Bentham! While Mill measures quantity *and* quality of pleasure, Bentham was focused more on just the quantity of pleasure. Which TV programmes generate lots of pleasure despite being of poor quality?

After teaching students the basics of higher (intellectual and moral) and lower (physical) pleasures, they need a stimulus to consider what this might look like in reality. A perfect resource for this is a copy of *Radio Times*. TV listings can provide a fascinating range of viewing options.

- Which programmes would John Stuart Mill consider to be an 'intellectually stimulating' way to spend the evening?
- Which channels would Mill consider to be concerned with 'animal pleasures'?

This can be good fun and memorable for students; however, it also brings Mill's discussion to the real world and opens up some of the nuances of his categories. Some programmes or channels fit an obvious category; which ones do not?

Other alternative ways of doing this would be with a magazine shelf or counter in a shop, or perhaps a collection of films currently on at the cinema.

Resources

Part 7

Which Bible to use?

'I used the NIV when doing my own A level and the NRSV at university – I like to use these as a teacher.'

One of the most frequently asked questions about the Bible is, 'Which is the best translation?' For the RE teacher, the question should be, 'Which is the best translation for the classroom?'

Here are short summaries of the main translations, ordered by suitability for age (age suggestions come from the Bible Society).

New International Reader's Version (NIRV)

(7+): Published in 1996, it follows a similar style to the New International Version (NIV), but in a more accessible and easy-to-read format. It can seem more interpretative than accurate in places, and some are put off by its low reading age.

Good News Bible (GNB)

(12+): Published in 1976, it is colloquial in places and attempts to be accessible to the reader. It has the addition of line drawings to help, but sometimes it goes far from the original text and doesn't include the full depth of the original Greek.

New International Version (NIV)

(12+): Published in 1978, and updated in 2011, it attempts to find a balance between staying very close to the text while communicating meaning as clearly as possible. It is easy to read, and the recent version introduces gender-neutral language, but some people find it bland and lacking in poetry.

New Revised Standard Version (NRSV)

(**16+**): Published in 1989 with the aim of being as literal as possible, apart from where this makes the meaning unclear. The Old Testament reflects Jewish interpretations, which raises questions when linking to Messianic prophecies. It aims to reduce male-only language.

King James Version (KJV)

(**17+**): Published in 1611 with a close literal translation. It has beautiful poetic language and has resulted in many phrases from the Bible becoming commonplace in the English language (for example, 'out of the mouths of babes' or 'the blind lead the blind'). Yet the meanings of certain words have changed over time, causing confusion.

Taking it further

Find out more about each version and further versions via the Bible Society.

A calendar of festivals

'I love my Shap calendar; it's next to my desk so I can always check what is coming up this month.'

These calendars are useful for much more than just classroom walls!

Taking it further

Are there any similarities across religions? Do they have festivals for similar reasons and at similar times? New Year celebrations? Festivals connected to light? Using a whole-year overview can make this much easier! Why are some festivals totally unique? What is the story behind them?

The Shap Working Party on World Religions in Education was set up in 1969 to help broaden the study of RE to include more faiths. This mission continues today and the organisation still publishes an annual calendar of religious festivals. The group is named after their initial meeting place, Shap, in Penrith.

The Shap calendar is usually available as an A2 wallchart that you can order, or as a downloadable A4 document. You can order the calendar from www.shapcalendar.org.uk. It is widely regarded as the most accurate and comprehensive list of religious festivals available, and is used by many organisations across the UK and beyond.

How can I use it?

For a start, they're useful for classroom walls! These can be extended to a monthly or termly display highlighting the key religious events coming up too.

Many RE teachers use the calendar for planning assemblies if they have this responsibility. They can also be used to ensure you are fully informed about the lives of the students in your school (for example, if you have a largely Muslim school population).

You may want to look at schemes of work and see when it is best to study certain topics and religions, so there is a link between your lessons and key dates and festivals.

Buying RE artefacts

'My students always love getting to see and hold the artefacts.'

No RE department is complete without a set of religious artefacts. If they are on display all year round, even better! They always provide fantastic discussion and help bring lessons to life.

Here are some ideas for how to source artefacts.

Professional suppliers: if your budget allows, there are a variety of companies that will provide a 'religion in a box', as it were. This is an easy way to stock up, but often one of the most expensive.

Loans: some county library services or education services offer loan services where you can book out a box of artefacts. This can be low cost, sometimes free.

Online: sites like eBay can often be a good source of secondhand or cheap artefacts. Even from overseas with postage, items can be very affordable. Obviously, check how your school will pay you back! You can build up unique, bespoke and absolutely fascinating collections.

Road trip: a day out in a city like Leicester can prove a worthwhile experience (especially if coupled with a visit to a few places of worship, or as a school trip). Items can be easily and cheaply bought from authentic and genuine sources. You could also ask friends who are going on holiday to do some shopping for you!

Local communities: asking local communities can result in a range of donations. Many faith communities will have unused items that they will often be happy to donate to local schools. Some faith communities may even send a speaker to present a donation.

> **Teaching tip**
>
> Make sure you know how your school procurement process works so that you are able to reclaim money spent on the artefacts, especially if using alternative sources!

Storing and using artefacts

'I sometimes forget that these are not just teaching resources, but genuine articles of faith for believers – some of whom are in my class!'

Artefacts are really useful as teaching tools and a key feature of most RE departments. However, storing and using them can cause problems, particularly as they are objects of devotion for religious believers.

Storing artefacts

Ensure the artefacts are not kept in a location where they can be accessed by students. Students could see it as funny to use them inappropriately, or they could simply be stolen or damaged. A department inventory is also useful and allows for items to be replaced as necessary.

Displaying artefacts

Some schools have display cabinets that allow artefacts to be on show outside of the lesson. This may be in the RE department or school library or another space. Other classrooms have shelves, although often these are too high to do the artefacts justice. Do not feel it is necessary to have them out at all times – often they are safer packed away. Remember that even when artefacts are replicas of the original, it is only appropriate they are handled with care and respect.

Using artefacts

Artefacts can be used in many ways:

- **Discussion:** what is this? What is it used for?
- **Philosophical enquiry:** do artefacts contain 'power'? How should we treat these items?
- **Cross-curricular links:** when was this first used (history)? Where does this come from (geography)?

The odd one out game

'Students love the inquisitive nature of this game. I've used it to great effect time and time again!' (*Claire Clinton*)

Ask students which artefact or object is the odd one out and why. It's possible that each one could be the odd one out for different but equally valid reasons!

This idea works really well if you have a good selection of artefacts and religious objects available. If you don't, it can easily be done with images displayed on the projector, or with a set of prepared cards.

Taking it further

Some classes with good prior knowledge might be able to complete a trio of items, if only given two – a third being similar to the first two.

Select four religious artefacts or objects and ask students to discuss which is the odd one out. Depending on the class, you could prepare some questions to help guide the discussion.

For example, your four artefacts could be:

- A Jewish kippah (a white and gold male prayer cap; a head covering showing humility before God).
- Sikh kacchera (white cotton Sikh underwear; worn by men and women once baptised as a sign of modesty).
- A hijab (white and blue cloth; a head covering for Muslim women, a sign of modesty).
- A nun's veil (black and white headdress, again showing modesty).

The discussion could include:

- Three objects have two colours each, so the odd one out is the Sikh shorts as they just have one colour.
- Three objects are worn on the head, so the odd one out is the Sikh shorts as they're not worn on the head.
- Three objects are worn for modesty reasons, so the odd one out is the Jewish kippah as it's worn out of respect for God.

Using tablets in RE

'I've been given a set of tablets for the department. How do I use them?'

Many teachers find tablets can help to engage students and produce really positive lessons.

Like any technology in the classroom, with tablets it's important to carefully consider effective uses and the opportunity cost of implementation. They're not cheap for schools to purchase and often departments will be asked to report on how they use them.

Quizzing: if you want to test students in 'exam conditions' but online, using tablets can be an easy way to do this. There are also lots of apps to carry out live, competitive quizzes, which can be useful as starters or to gauge levels of understanding at the end of a topic (Kahoot! is one example).

Collaborative work: students can work on projects collaboratively, for example, in Google Slides. Different students can be given different parts of the project to work on.

Recording: tablets can record both sound and video, and come with apps for editing. This can allow students to document more creative work and share it more widely. Many schools even share videos on social media, which could help promote the department.

Scripture: if you don't have access to classroom sets of Bibles, Qur'ans or other holy books, then these are all available via free apps.

Using social media feeds

'Students spend hours a day on social media; can any of it be useful to their studies?'

There are a huge number of people and organisations on social media that have views on topics linked to RE. Here are some ideas for how to use this rich resource.

First, check if you can get on social media at school! If you can't, you can screengrab social media posts at home to use in lessons. Look for posts that can back up (or challenge) viewpoints in the classroom.

If students can access social media at school, consider asking them to find posts linked to a topic that you're studying, such as stewardship. Can they find an example of an opinion on stewardship from a well-known religious leader or organisation? What about examples of people acting as good stewards? Do 'real life' social media posts contradict or support traditional teachings?

Here's an example when studying stewardship. Check out the following organisations' websites or social media feeds: The CoE Environment Department, A Rocha UK, Muslim Hands, and HKCA (Hindu Kush Conservation Association).

If studying humanitarian aid and/or helping the poor, check out: The Tzu Chi Foundation, CAFOD, Nishkam SWAT, Muslim Aid, and The Apostleship of the Sea.

Teaching tip

Be very careful about giving students lesson time on social media; they will find it very difficult to avoid distraction! Also, consider whether you want them to interact on social media. A critical or inappropriate comment on their part could backfire and cause a variety of problems for them and you.

Taking it further

Do social media posts from religious leaders such as the Pope or Dalai Lama provide a source of wisdom and authority? Do you think they write the tweets themselves? Does it matter?

Using a visualiser

'I wanted to model my thinking to the students. I wanted to show them how I would construct an answer.'

It's a familiar teaching technique to produce a complete model answer for students to use, but these can be quite daunting to many. Often students benefit from the step-by-step guidance that can be provided by modelling.

Sometimes modelling is possible via simply writing on the board. I've sometimes typed as I talk. However, I've found the best way to do it is as close as possible to the experience of the student. That means using pen, paper and a projection onto the board.

Many teachers first used visualisers to simply display good work. However, I've found them far more useful when used to project a live stream of my writing. This can be done via relatively inexpensive visualisers, or wirelessly with a tablet.

Metacognition (which is an important part of modelling) is defined as an 'awareness and understanding of one's own thought processes'. This is often the difference between the expert and the novice. Quite literally, how do you produce a critically analytical and evaluative essay in RE?

Talk through your thought processes aloud: what are you doing and why? What are you choosing to include? What are you leaving out? Why have you picked that phrase? Why have you put things in that order?

It is possible that some of your more able students could do this live modelling too, though it is often worth prepping them in advance!

Teaching Humanism

'Their website is packed with lots of top-quality teaching resources which can save us hours. In addition, they can provide free guest speakers.'

Invite students to research Humanism and compare Humanists and theists.

Humanists UK (www.understandinghumanism. org.uk) is generally regarded as the best educational resource for studying non-religious worldviews. It provides a whole range of materials including videos and presentations, and also sends trained speakers into schools.

It is worth noting that many thinkers who have identified as Humanists did not label themselves as such, but their beliefs might be described as broadly Humanist. Some lived at times when atheism simply wasn't accepted; others before Humanism had been fully defined.

Key Humanist thinkers

Get students to research some of the following people: David Hume, Mary Wollstonecraft, Charles Darwin, John Stuart Mill, George Eliot or Bertrand Russell. Why would they be considered Humanist?

Defining 'Humanism'

Humanists UK define Humanists as people who:

- reject the idea of the supernatural
- make ethical decisions based on reason, empathy, and a concern for living beings
- believe that human beings can act to give their own lives meaning by seeking happiness in this life.

Get students to highlight and identify what makes a Humanist different to a theist, but also what is similar.

Teaching tip

Often non-religious worldviews are simply taught as a comparison or alternative to religious views; however, some schools are now teaching the topic as a distinct approach, comparable to a faith. Would it be useful to get a Humanist speaker on a 'faith debate' panel? This may be an appropriate approach in your school.

IDEA 47

Food in RE

'My students loved the lesson where they got to eat!'

This idea gives some suggestions of foods you could introduce to your students.

Taking it further

Many religions either have food laws (such as kosher in Judaism or halal in Islam), or food traditions (such as no meat on a Friday for Catholics). Find out what they are and what their background is.

Food plays a key role in many religious traditions. It is also often easily available, sometimes even in your local supermarket!

Seder (Judaism): the Passover meal is often replicated in the RE classroom. The ingredients are usually readily available or can be substituted for similar items. Seder dishes can be bought cheaply, with some websites now even offering disposable versions.

Iftar (Islam): this could be as simple as providing some dates, as shared by many Muslims when they break their fast during Ramadan. However, there are often public iftars where you could take a small group of students, depending on your local area.

Langar (Sikhism): if there is a gurdwara nearby, taking a group of students to visit will enable them to take part in the vegetarian community meal provided for all (regardless of religion, caste, gender, economic status or ethnicity).

Mithai (Hinduism): these sweets are readily available in areas with a Hindu community around Diwali. They are exchanged among friends and family, and a Hindu student may even bring them in for their friends.

Bonus idea ★

Why not use food on open evening to ensure lots of visitors to the department?

Start with a picture

'Students often have bits and pieces of background knowledge – this can remind them of what they do already know.'

As the saying goes, a picture is worth a thousand words. Getting students to analyse an image can work well as a starter, but equally could be used as a task to consolidate or apply learning.

Give students an image to analyse: images can vary from classic and famous works of religious art to more contemporary images. The six Ws could be displayed on the board, or maybe you want students to focus on just a couple of questions depending on the topic or image. The six Ws are a really useful set of questions; you could point out to students that they are quite often used by journalists, in research and even by the police! This is a really popular starter in my own department.

Teaching tip

If this activity works well, why not have the questions up on the wall so you just need the image in your presentation?

- **Who?** Who can you see? What do you notice about their appearance? Who is in the background?
- **What?** What is going on? Is it a particular event or moment? What objects do you notice?
- **Where?** Where does this take place? Does this location match your understanding of the event? Is it familiar or unknown?
- **When?** Does the picture match the timeline of the actual event? How do you know? What are the clues?
- **Why?** Is there a reason the artist has chosen to complete this piece of artwork? Is it a representation of their personal faith? Why is this event important to them?
- **How?** How do you know? Justify your responses!

Dealing with loose paper

'I love to create a worksheet, but my students end up with really messy exercise books!'

Many RE teachers love creating worksheets or printing off interesting news stories or articles. The problem is what to do with them! This is especially problematic if you are an RE teacher who sees a large number of students; the last thing you need when checking books is loose paper!

Teaching tip

Once you have found your ideal routine that works with your preferred 'how', break it down into a few clear steps and ensure it is displayed to students every time during their first term. Put in on the board, on the wall, or even in their books!

It's worth drilling a routine from the start! Have a really clear system for ensuring things are stuck in, and do it that way every time. Who gives out the glue or sticky tape? Who collects it? How long are students given? And importantly, how do you want papers to be stuck in?

- One option is to stick papers in so they are like an extra page (glue or sticky tape down one edge so it opens like a page).
- Hole punching has become more popular recently. Each book is hole punched and then treasury tags are used on the sheets (which also need hole punching!).
- Consider A4+ books. These are just a little bigger than your sheets, which really helps to reduce the tatty edges sticking out!

Other options:

- Some RE teachers like to produce booklets instead of books, but consider if producing these is the best use of your time.
- Other RE teachers love using ring binders – students can easily fill them with all the sheets they like!

Using longer articles and essays

'Using this method, students were able to navigate around longer articles with ease.'

The use of original and extended texts is really useful in RE, especially at GCSE and A level. Even longer prayers like the Creed or the Shema can pose problems to students and teachers trying to pinpoint where you are up to. Here are a few ideas to make using longer texts easier.

Number the lines

Many holy books have verse numbers so readers can make direct references to small bits of text, which could be as short as two words (such as John 11:35, 'Jesus wept'). Some documents, such as those published by the Vatican, number each paragraph.

Recreating this for the text you are using is an easy way to direct students to the exact bits they require. It can also be useful for their own notes. The 'numbered list' function in Word works, but may require a bit of manual work – there are websites that can do it for you.

Text in the middle of a page

As well as changing the line spacing of the text to at least 1.5, or even double, it's important to create space to annotate the text. Photocopying an A4 sheet into the middle of an A3 sheet works, or just resize the sheet before printing.

Pre-reading, rereading and silent reading

Don't be afraid of reading! Colleagues in English will expect periods of extended reading in their lessons, and we should be unafraid of doing the same. This could take place in the lesson or outside it.

Teaching tip

Spend some time annotating your own copy of the text first, highlighting the things you want to refer to – otherwise you will be annoyed you missed something!

Wider reading

'I used to tell my A level students I wanted them to do wider reading, but never really specified what that was, and then I was surprised when they didn't do any.'

The idea of independent, self-motivated and self-directed students is the dream for many RE teachers. We hope they develop a natural love of the subject and can automatically navigate the huge wealth of information available to them. You'd never consider telling a KS3 student to simply 'read around' a topic, but by A level and even GCSE we expect them to have developed this skill!

Here are some ideas for helping students develop this skill.

Search terms

Ensure students know how to search the internet properly. For example, if you want them to read around the Design Argument, they might find it helpful to add 'A level' to their search. This will help to make sure the information that comes up is tailored to their level. Likewise, for GCSE students who are just starting to learn about the Design Argument, it might help to search for 'Design Argument introduction' or 'Design Argument basics'.

Reading lists

Create reading lists that students can access and use in their own time. These don't have to be just limited to books; I've created lists of news articles, PDFs, websites, and as I've checked every one, I can confidently tell students that *everything* is of use!

Just reading?

Videos can be just as useful, as can podcasts. Again curation is key here; there is lots of rubbish that students could easily spend their time with.

Knowledge organisers

'Every topic I teach now has a knowledge organiser. It's the basics. If you don't know this, you will find it hard to get to grips with the key questions at the heart of this area of study.'

A 'knowledge organiser' is a document that outlines the key facts and information that students need to know in order to have a basic knowledge and understanding of a topic. It can be used in a variety of ways.

I try to keep my knowledge organisers to one side of A4, but some teachers are happy with two sides. A simple, universal format can be helpful, although this is not always possible where religions or topics don't fit a comparable framework. A common one would have: key words, dates, people, and stories. Knowledge organisers can be used in different ways, for example:

At the start of a topic: if you provide the knowledge organiser at the start of a topic, students then have a reference point for everything that is to come. They can keep referring to it to see where new knowledge fits in. Homework can be based around learning certain sections.

As a focus for quizzing: some teachers simply quiz using the knowledge organiser, and students can easily correct answers by using their own.

As recall practice: provide a blank copy of the knowledge organiser for students to see what they can reproduce from memory.

To summarise a unit: students can complete their own knowledge organisers at the end of a topic.

Teaching tip

When planning as a department, agreeing what the key information should be for a topic in RE can end up being controversial, but the debate and discussion can be useful CPD. For example, what are the essentials of Sikhism that should go on the knowledge organiser?

Reduce, reuse, recycle

'It's easy to create work for yourself when actually you don't need to.'

Here are three key principles used by A. J. Smith, an RE teacher, for making lesson resources and presentations simpler to prepare and use.

Teaching tip

At KS3, I use a really simple colour scheme matched to the textbooks (e.g. Year 7 slides are blue, Year 8 slides are green), and even at A level the different paper components match their lesson resources (e.g. philosophy is light blue). This is as helpful to me as it is to the students!

Reduce: reduce the amount of information down to just what is required. Be clear on exactly what students need to know and don't confuse or distract from that by having too much additional material. If your resource looks crowded then it needs to be spread over more than one page or slide – or something needs to be cut!

Reuse: reuse the same key terms and associated icons across every single resource. Choose one icon to represent stewardship and stick to it in the PowerPoint, booklet, worksheets and knowledge organiser. The familiarity of these things will help to reduce the cognitive load on students and help them to learn and work with the key terms far more efficiently.

Recycle: use the same visual style every single lesson, and ensure it is a simple one! When students look at your resources they should be focused on the information and not the fonts or colours (or animations!), and recycling the same templates ensures this is the case. It is also a huge time saver.

Work out where you do need to spend your time, but use these three principles to help reduce workload and actually make your lessons more effective (a double win!).

The RE-Definitions app

'I knew the word, but I didn't know how to pronounce it!'

RE-Definitions is an app and website produced by CTVC. It provides easy and simple access to the pronunciation and meaning of more than 200 key terms for RE.

As an app on mobiles and tablets, and as a website on PCs, RE-Definitions is for anyone who wants to understand key religious words and be able to pronounce them with confidence.

How to use it?

For teachers:

- Practise pronouncing words before the lesson. The way you say it will be the way they say it! Practise as a class too.
- Get students to learn a set of words for a religion or topic and test their knowledge (and pronunciation skills!) in class.
- Plan for more oracy-based lessons – with debates or speeches – using students' greater confidence to pronounce the words.

For students:

- Refer to the words to help build vocabulary and technical language for answers.
- Create flashcards to self-test the words.
- Work in pairs or a group to test understanding, where one person plays the word and the other person has to define it.

Teaching tip

If you have a set of class tablets, ensure the app is downloaded. Do your school PCs have a favourites or bookmarks list? Add the site!

The app is available from the Apple App Store or Google Play Store, or online at www.re-definitions.org.uk.

Interest and engagement

Part 8

Managing a visitor

'A visitor to the classroom brings alive the work that goes on in the classroom. They are a living, breathing example of what it means to be a member of that faith community.'

Inviting a visiting speaker into the RE classroom is both an exciting and daunting prospect. When it goes well, it can really enhance student learning and offer a great opportunity to ask questions.

Taking it further

Why not consider an inter-faith event where you invite a number of speakers on one day? You could have a panel debate with questions prepared by students.

Planning the visit

Do your research and make sure you get the right person to come in and speak. Can you ask for recommendations from other local schools or could your SACRE help? It is reasonable to ask a prospective speaker what schools they have worked with before. Make sure you also check your school visitor policy and communicate this to the speaker. Check for any pastoral issues with the students involved (particularly if it's a sensitive topic, such as euthanasia or abortion) and brief any other staff involved.

Before the visit

Plan the session together and ensure the speaker is fully informed about what is being asked of them. Some things to clarify:

- **Timings:** agree on arrival times, the length of the talk, the total length of the session and roughly when they are going to be departing.
- **Content:** make sure they will stick to the agreed topics and cover the material that you need them to. Remind the speaker of the students' level of knowledge and discuss how the speaker will deliver the session (for example, a talk, or questions and answers).

- **Equipment:** the speaker may want audiovisual equipment, and asking for presentations or videos in advance can help avoid technical difficulties.

Ask to see materials in advance to ensure they are suitable and appropriate. Check, and clarify, who the speaker represents within the faith.

The day of the visit

Ensure the school reception knows to expect the visitor and work out who will meet them. Remember, you can't be in two places at once, settling and preparing students and meeting the guest. Offer refreshments and always have a glass of water ready!

During the visit

Be ready! Something may need clarifying, or the talk could go off track. The organiser, rather than the speaker, needs to be in control of this. The speaker will want reassurance that the school is in charge of behaviour and will intervene if necessary for any reason.

After the visit

Write a short letter or card of thanks. This could be written by yourself or a group of students. Include some positive comments from students or staff. Complete follow-up work with students to ensure the experience is captured.

> **Bonus idea** ★
>
> Inter-Faith Week takes place during the week after Remembrance Sunday each November. This is a great opportunity to invite in a speaker or run an inter-faith event and get some positive local press coverage.

A virtual pilgrimage

'Pilgrimage is a very ancient tradition, but with the use of modern technology, places from around the world are just a few clicks away!'

A visit to a local place of worship is always a fantastic experience for students. However, it is also possible to visit key religious sites around the world for free!

Teaching tip

After learning about a place of pilgrimage, it may be useful consolidation to ask students to explore a virtual pilgrimage site for their homework. Picking a specific link and sharing it with them is always a good idea.

Taking it further

After experiencing a virtual pilgrimage, students could attempt to make their own virtual pilgrimages for each other to explore, from photos and videos they can readily find on the internet.

Using digital maps, within minutes students can be transported around the world to the Golden Temple in Amritsar, then on to the Great Mosque in Mecca and St Peter's in Rome. Google Street View has even managed to take images inside some of these places to give an intimate and detailed experience. Alternatively, the ability to transform mobile phones into virtual reality headsets gives access to 360° and 3D videos posted to YouTube.

However, careful consideration is needed to ensure that students get the most out of the experience. It may also be limited by access to technology within the school. A demonstration via the whiteboard from the teacher's computer could be the most effective and efficient use of the technology.

Another useful way of viewing places of significance virtually is to search for live webcams, for example, at the Western Wall, on the grotto in Lourdes, or above the Kaaba. This is helpful for students to see the 'living' nature of these places.

It's also worth remembering that many Christians have been carrying out 'virtual pilgrimages' for a very long time via the Stations of the Cross, which is a recreation of the Via Dolorosa ('Way of Suffering') In Jerusalem.

Contact a religious believer

'My students loved the authenticity of speaking to a religious believer via email. It gave a great purpose to their question-writing.'

The ideal situation is to arrange for a visiting speaker to come in person to the school, but in reality this is often challenging and logistically difficult! Times, locations, multiple classes... with the best of intentions, it can be very difficult.

Some SACREs can provide speakers, or you may have developed good local relationships; however, for many RE teachers, local communities of other faiths can be small, or far away. Technology can be used effectively to provide an alternative approach.

Video conferencing

If you are able to find a contact, using web-based chat software can be effective. This can even be broadcast in a larger space, such as a hall. It is worth preparing questions in advance and nominating students to ask specific questions.

Email a believer

RE: Online (www.reonline.org.uk) provides a service whereby students or teachers can email a believer with their questions and get a response. They cover a variety of mainstream faiths and beliefs, including Humanism, but also smaller religious groups such as Bahá'í, The Church of Jesus Christ of Latter-day Saints, and Paganism.

Students are encouraged to introduce themselves with a few words about who they are and why they are writing.

Teaching tip

Instead of getting your whole class to email a religious believer individually, it's best to collate the questions to select the best few. This can be done via class discussion, refining and improving the questions and sending them off collectively.

Using news articles

'RE is always in the news, and this helps students to understand the subject's importance in the world.'

If you often watch or read the news and think to yourself, 'This will be excellent for when I am teaching...', you are not alone! However, working out how best to use news stories in the classroom requires a bit of preparation.

When you're looking at which news stories to use, think about the following things:

- **Bias:** does the media source have any particular bias? Often this will be subtle and implicit. Be careful of not adding in additional biases of your own!
- **Accuracy:** is the religious content accurate? Are key terms used in the right way?
- **Issue:** is this actually a religious issue? Is it really a cultural or political issue? (And if so, do you have time for it in the RE curriculum?)
- **Agenda:** what is the aim behind the media a) sharing the story and b) sharing it in the way they have?

It's often better if you find articles for your students to digest. However, getting students to look through the 'Religion' category on news websites can also be an interesting and useful exercise. Setting this for homework before a lesson can help to engage students in the topic before you even begin!

> **Bonus idea** ★
>
> An 'RE in the news' display that is updated weekly can be a fantastic addition to the classroom or RE corridor.

RE in the news

'It's not "*when* RE is in the news", it's more like "*when* RE is *not* in the news"!'

Create a bank of articles that you update regularly, but be careful not to let the news dictate your weekly lessons.

Using the news in RE is a really useful to way to help students see the relevance of the subject and engage with it in a real and tangible way. Yet it is important to get the balance right, as you shouldn't end up with a curriculum that is completely dictated by the news!

Save them up!

Add links to schemes of work in relevant places so that you can bring up the news story when you get an appropriate point. If this is an ongoing process, with regular updating, the news stories will not get too out of date. Although some will last you for years!

Five-minute update

You could have a rota with one student allocated to share a piece of RE in the news from the week that's just gone. Just be careful if doing this at the start of the lesson as it could easily spill over into other teaching time.

Quote posters

'I want my students to be immersed in the key quotes they need; some are useful for many different areas!'

Quotes have always been useful in RE, and learning them is nothing new. However, they have become more valuable at GCSE level as additional marks are now available for including sources of wisdom and authority. A 'quote poster' can help students to learn these key quotes.

A 'quote poster' is one way of livening up classrooms, corridors and even exercise-book covers! You can involve students in aspects of quote selection, creation and placement around the school.

Software that you could use to create a poster includes:

- Apps like Word Swag: it turns your words into photo-text designs.
- Websites such as Canva: a simple graphic design website.
- Programmes such as Photoshop (although a bit more know-how is needed for this!).

Consider things such as:

- Whether images are in copyright or not (there are various free sites to use such as Pixabay and Unsplash).
- Lightening or darkening images to make the quotes sitting on top of them more readable.
- Picking suitable fonts and font sizes so that quotes can be read easily.
- The resolution of images and text if you plan to print A4 or A3 (or bigger!); will it just look pixelated?

Careers with RE

'I never realised how many opportunities there are for RE students!'

Most RE teachers will have heard a number of students say, 'What's the point in RE? I don't want to be a vicar!' Introducing your students to careers that benefit from the study of RE can help to engage their interest in the subject.

Those who teach Religious Studies at GCSE or A level are never surprised that the subject is so popular with young people. Both the subject matter and the critical and analytical approach taken towards it help to equip students with the skills, knowledge and attitudes necessary to succeed in modern Britain.

Make sure your students know about the value of studying RE for further study and employment. For example:

- RE gives students opportunities to discuss and debate complex and sometimes difficult topics, issues and texts.
- Students can find a sense of confirmation through grappling academically and philosophically with their faith (or lack of faith).
- Students often feel that RE helps them develop their understanding of the beliefs, values and worldviews of others.

Where next?

RS degrees – the natural progression for many from GCSE and A level RS – allow students to enter a wide range of careers. Some may choose to teach the subject, but journalism, civil service and even law are common destinations. RE studies help journalists because they develop the skills of analysis and evaluation, especially around complex sources of information.

Teaching tip

There are some valuable case studies on people who have studied RS and how it has helped them at http://casestudies.reonline.org.uk.

Taking it further

Past students could record their experience of continuing to study RS beyond the school, explaining why they enjoy it and what the benefits are.

Bonus idea ★

Why not get students to research famous people and celebrities with RS degrees? You could create a display in your classroom featuring these people, alongside RS-related careers.

Be the philosopher

'What would Dawkins say to that?'

Sixth-form students can spend a lot of time learning about certain key scholars who feature in a range of different topics. Using name badges, or even masks, students can take on the role of the scholar in question and argue for their view during class debate.

Taking it further

You could pre-select some topics and allow students to pick and prepare their own character. They need to argue their view as the discussion develops.

This activity only works well if students really know the scholars and what they would say. Start with the topics the scholars are most commonly associated with before getting students to think about other issues.

- Put students into groups of four.
- Allocate a scholar to each student in the group: Thomas Aquinas, Richard Swinburne, Richard Dawkins and A. J. Ayer often work well. Allocate your scholars carefully: it is a great opportunity to differentiate!
- Start by debating statements such as 'God is the designer of the universe' or 'God is the uncaused causer'.
- To help students think more creatively, pick a topic that some of the scholars clearly haven't said anything about, such as 'IVF is wrong' or 'Christians should recycle'.

Investigations

'Students love to take on an investigation. They can end up being long-lived too!'

Religion is everywhere, but sometimes students don't notice. Giving them a task of investigating and recording the religion that they see in their day-to-day lives can really help them appreciate the importance of religious knowledge.

A general investigation

Give students the scenario that religion has now been banned in this country, and ask them to record any evidence of this law being broken as a homework task. Encourage them to look for religious symbols worn by people, buildings, signs, mentions of festivals (Christmas or Easter), links to religious laws (kosher or halal food), phrases used in conversation ('oh my God' or 'bless you'), TV programmes, music, and so on. They will end up with a long list!

A specific investigation

Ask colleagues in January to donate their Christmas cards. You should end up with a large box! Get students to identify which ones contain a religious image. They should be able to do this quite quickly.

You could also collect newspapers and get students to go through them and identify which stories contain a reference to religion.

Taking it further

An analysis of religious knowledge in the media can be an interesting investigation to carry out. Does the press know what they are talking about? Can you find references to religion that are generalised or even inaccurate?

The disciplines of RE

'Introducing the complexity and diversity of the subject is a fantastic way to get students engaged – there is something for everyone!'

Look at different subject disciplines that are linked to RE with your students, from anthropology to theology, and introduce the idea of different disciplinary perspectives.

Teaching tip

It is commonly agreed that no RE curriculum should be too focused on just one of these disciplines. Does your curriculum have a spread and balance? Do you need to audit it to check?

Taking it further

Find out about Exeter University's RE-searchers Approach (www.ltlre.org/projects/my-first-project-leaders) or the 'balanced RE' approach. These should underpin the whole RE curriculum and its teaching.

With RE being a relatively new subject, it borrows and makes use of a variety of other subject disciplines. Until the late 19th century, theology would have been the subject discipline closest to RE. Yet even within theology, there are a variety of different approaches.

Religious Education or Religious Studies can be studied through a broad set of principles, approaches and methods of enquiry. It is worth highlighting these to students:

- anthropology
- sociology
- psychology
- philosophy
- history (of religion)
- theology.

Get students to find out a little about these different disciplines (and their etymology!). Then pick a topic like 'miracles'. Ask students to approach their enquiry through the different disciplines: what would a psychologist be looking at and why? What might a theologian ask? When it comes to a topic like the Reformation, theologians would ask very different questions from historians or social scientists!

The art of storytelling

'It is absolutely vital that RE teachers are really good at this!'

Human beings love stories. We generally prefer narrative to logical propositions, and this is also true in the classroom.

When teaching A level, sometimes little stories about the theologians and philosophers help students to connect with them. For example, discussion of A. J. Ayer's supposed death-bed conversion can reinforce his logical positivist stance.

Good stories have the ability to stick in the long-term memory. Matthew Dell, Senior Lecturer, St Mary's University, suggests a way of strengthening this is to get pupils to retell the stories they learn in class to their families.

The first challenge is to find a story that serves the purpose of the lesson. Sometimes this story can be drawn from personal experience, but in the traditions of the major religions there are rich seams of stories. From the lives of religious founders such as Jesus, Muhammad and Guru Nanak, there are many examples of stories that can be used to aid learning.

The RE teacher needs to be a gifted storyteller because when you tell a good story, not only do you have your students' undivided attention, students often remember the details better as well.

So how do you tell a good story? Practise and rehearse it; commit it largely to memory; use flash cards or even a script to help as prompts. Use your voice, facial expressions and gestures to play different parts or get the meaning across. Develop a sense of rhythm and timing so you can build to a climax. Use humour.

Teaching tip

Consider ways in which students can record a story in their book. Summarising in bullet points seems simple but does require practice and not all students will find it easy.

Taking it further

Why not use artefacts to help tell the story?

Bonus idea ★

Students often enjoy presenting stories to one another. Some teachers enjoy dramatic or artistic presentations too!

Parking questions

'My students have so many questions and want to discuss everything. We never finish the lesson!'

It can be difficult to judge genuine excitement and interest in a topic — are students' questions just a distraction? You could delay answering a student's question. If that question is so important, you can return to it a little later. It is vital that RE teachers have mechanisms for recording and answering questions later.

Recording questions

Use the margin: get students to jot down any questions they have in the margin. Often you will answer them anyway later in the lesson, or they will become unimportant.

Use sticky notes: if it is the kind of lesson that will naturally generate a lot of questions (sex, death, etc.), get students to write them down, collect them and then answer the most frequently occurring ones.

Ration questions: for students who naturally ask lots of questions, a scrap piece of paper or the back of their book can give them the space to note down a larger volume of questions. Ask the student to pick the one question they would really like answering.

Answering questions

Sometimes with the best will in the world, you will not get time to answer all the questions. You could turn unanswered questions into a homework task: perhaps pick three from the class that have not been answered and get all students to research and write answers to them.

Philosophy film club

'It's brilliant. Everyone wants to get to philosophy film club!'

A philosophy film club is a good way of igniting that spark of love for RE. It can be part of a wider strategy to boost take-up of the subject at GCSE and A level.

A philosophy film club can help students to discuss the philosophical and ethical issues that come out of lessons, as well as developing their religious knowledge. It can also help them to spot how much religion has influenced our culture. It's a good way of finding the theologians of the future too.

Nikki McGee, RE teacher and Head of Philosophy, Religions and Ethics at a school in Dorset, successfully runs a philosophy film club. It runs once a half term for KS3 and once a half term for KS4/5. Invites are emailed to students, but the club is also advertised on Twitter and in the school bulletin.

> 'We meet after school. We provide popcorn and drinks. We watch the film and then discuss it afterwards picking up the main themes.'

For each half term there is a long list of films to choose from and the students vote for their favourites using an online questionnaire. The club is very popular with parents, who often send thank-you emails and suggestions for future films.

- For KS3, previous films have included *Little Buddha*, *Gandhi*, *My Sister's Keeper*, *Life of Pi* and *Narnia*.
- For KS4/5, previous films have included *Dead Man Walking*, *The Matrix*, *Juno* and *Minority Report*.

Teaching tip

After the film, students could write a review of the film linking it to RE lessons. This can then be published in the school newsletter or on the school website.

Taking it further

As well as using popular films, for KS4/5 challenging documentaries could also be included.

Ethical dilemmas

'If you want to get the class discussing a topic, presenting an ethical dilemma at the start of the lesson can be a good place to begin.'

Discussing topical and/or real-life situations in class can help students make connections between their RE studies and real life.

Teaching tip

Ensure there is enough time to discuss and listen to students' answers and questions (perhaps don't finish the lesson like this!).

Ethical dilemmas, by their very nature, provide debate and potential disagreement. It's important to pick the scenario carefully and keep it linked to the topic being studied. Having a task that is linked to it as a follow-on is also important, so it doesn't just become an irrelevant hook.

Examples

- A Christian doctor has been sacked because he refused to carry out an abortion. Should he have been sacked?
- A Jewish person has been invited to dinner at a non-kosher restaurant with work colleagues. Should she go?
- A Sikh man has been asked to remove his kirpan by a security guard at an office block. Should he comply or refuse?

These do require religious knowledge and so could act as revision or consolidation tasks. Students may need further knowledge in order to answer, so research could form part of the task. Accepting that there is not one possible answer is important; in these examples, there are different possible ways for the situations to be resolved!

Go local

'Why would you *not* use local history, culture, geography, architecture and art in lessons?'

If you use your locally agreed syllabus, your schemes of work may already incorporate local links, but there's still a great opportunity to integrate these into your RE lessons.

To complement textbook images of a church or mosque, why not use images of a local place of worship? It creates instant engagement to see somewhere immediately recognisable. Even documenting a place which isn't local but which you've visited personally will hook students in ('Here I am in a temple I visited on holiday...'). Make sure you collect guidebooks and leaflets too.

Local current affairs and history can also be brought into lessons. Is your school near to the ruins of a monastery? That would be perfect for teaching about the Reformation. Do you teach in Cambridgeshire? When discussing animal rights, perhaps reference Stop Huntingdon Animal Cruelty. Teachers in East London can easily reference the 1889 dock strike when looking at the dignity of the worker.

Taking it further

If a trip to a place of worship is impossible, instead of using a video found online, why not create your own, by going in person to a place of worship and filming it yourself? If you have a media studies department, even better!

Bonus idea ★

Encourage students to bring in their own photos of their local place of worship... or of course their holiday snaps! It makes for a great classroom display.

University links

'What better way to inspire your students to choose degree-level RS? Visit the universities, but also get them to come to you!'

Develop a relationship with a university: the potential for collaboration is huge!

A requirement of charging higher tuition fees is a necessity to do outreach and access work. Therefore most universities will jump at the chance to work with schools. From a subject point of view, rather than going via the general access or engagement office, go straight to the faculty or department for religious studies. I've generally found them to be pleasantly surprised and open to suggestions.

Some university departments already offer open lectures as part of their open days, but there's nothing wrong with simply asking if you can attend a lecture or two with your class. Or ask them to come and deliver a session in your own school. Inviting undergraduates to speak to sixth formers can be mutually beneficial; not only do you get some additional input, you may even inspire the university students to consider a career in teaching!

Once you've developed a relationship with a university, asking for resources, access to libraries, and two-way visits may all be possible. And don't be surprised when your students decide they want to study at this department.

Bonus idea ★

Ask the university department to put on some CPD for your department. Teachers need to develop their knowledge too!

Patchwork thinking game

'I enjoyed this game, and even as an experienced RE teacher, it generated some interesting discussion and debate with colleagues!'

This is an idea shared by RE advisor Claire Clinton, who uses this thinking-skills game to draw on students' prior learning, getting them to make connections between the information.

This game can be used with any topic. It could be centred around one religion or a number of religions, and focus on philosophy, theology, history or religion.

You'll need to provide each small group of students with a selection of 20 cards. These cards could have facts, images or quotations from people or holy books on them, all linked in some way to your chosen topic.

Students then have to place 16 of these cards onto a 4x4 grid. Students can't add a card onto the grid unless they can give a reason for how it relates to all of the other cards it touches. If the group agrees with their reasons then the card can stay.

Encourage students to think about and challenge any wrong ideas around any of the connections they're making. Bring the class back together and ask students to share with a partner three things they've learnt from having done the activity.

Teaching tip

This can be used as a great revision activity.

Taking it further

For more of a challenge, enlarge the grid to 5x5 (25 squares) and give students 30 cards to choose from.

Concept lines

'A concept line is a useful strategy to get students to think through a concept or idea in a structured, discursive way.'

This is a technique that can be used effectively from Years 7 to 13. It involves giving every student a word or an image and asking them to choose where to place it on a scale.

Teaching tip

With a big class, this may be done in a number of smaller groups. Students could then go and view other groups' lines to see if they got the same outcomes.

Start by choosing a concept to explore, such as 'religion'. Select a number of words, phrases or images that help to unpack what that word means or doesn't mean.

Place a strip of masking tape down as a line on the floor. Label one end 'more...' and one end 'less...', for example, 'more religious' at one end and 'less religious' at the other end.

Some other words that this works well with are 'enlightened', 'moral', 'male/female' and 'shalom/peace'. You could also use any religion or worldview ('more Christian' and 'less Christian', for example).

Print out your selection of words and images so every student has one each. Then provide the ground rules:

- You can't show anyone (or talk to anyone about) your word or image.
- You should place your word or image on the line wherever you think it should be placed.
- You can't place your word or image on top of anything else.

Get the students to stand in a circle around the line, taking it in turns to place their items without speaking. At the end, students can ask to move something, justify their request, and then move it if the group agrees. The activity will help students to define and understand the concept or word you want them to focus on in your lesson.

Literacy and oracy

Part 9

A priori and a posteriori

'These two types of knowledge are key to any study of philosophy, yet my students often get confused.'

For students who are ready to embark on their first adventures into philosophy, these two phrases can cause confusion, especially as they are in Latin! Use these strategies with your students to remind them what the terms mean.

'From the earlier' (a priori) and 'from the later' (a posteriori) were popularised by Immanuel Kant, but have been used since the ancient Greeks. The best way to help students to understand these is to teach them in the context of synthetic and analytic statements, and inductive and deductive reasoning. They usually come together: a priori knowledge, analytic statements and deductive reasoning as one group and a posteriori knowledge, synthetic statements and inductive reasoning as the other.

What do you need to **get off your posterior** for?

Many students won't be familiar with their backside or buttocks being called their 'posterior', but it does help! You need to get off your backside and look at the evidence to draw conclusions with a posteriori knowledge. Demonstrate by asking a student to walk over to the window to check something going on outside.

What do you have **prior knowledge** of?

Knock off the 'i' and this can become easy for students. For example, I don't need to count two of something and then count another two to know 2 + 2 = 4. I don't have to get off my backside and investigate to find out the answer, as I have prior knowledge of this.

Now make up some examples of these two types of knowledge.

Active listening

'How do I get my students to listen better?'

RE by its very nature encourages students to share personal stories, feelings and emotions. If these are to be shared, it is vital that other students are engaged in active listening. This is also a useful classroom skill in general to ensure focus on the teacher.

One technique that was originally proposed in *Teach Like a Champion* by Doug Lemov, but has since been adapted in many ways by teachers, is 'SLANT'. There are many versions in circulation from different teachers and different schools, but the original is:

- **S**it up
- **L**isten
- **A**sk and answer questions
- **N**od your head
- **T**rack the speaker.

Some of the common variations replace 'Nod your head' with 'Note take'; some have added 'Nod and smile'. 'N' has also been replaced simply with 'No talking'. 'L' has also been replaced with 'Lead forward' or 'Look and give eye contact'.

These are very similar to active listening techniques suggested in coaching, and are useful for having conversations with colleagues.

It's important to introduce the idea of active listening to the class at the start of the year, and regularly reinforce it. Many teachers put a copy of the acronym on books or a poster. Over time, it can really help students to understand what is expected of them when listening in RE lessons. This can help to grow the confidence of others in the classroom to share their experiences and can help to enable effective classroom discussion.

Taking it further

This could form part of your introductory lesson. It could be framed around the idea of dialogue with religious people. Why is it important that we listen and how do we best do that?

Lemov, D (2015), *Teach Like a Champion*. San Francisco, CA: Jossey Bass.

Etymology

'I never thought chilli con carne would help with GCSE RS.'

In a subject that uses many terms that have close links to both Latin and Greek (particularly for Christianity), understanding etymology can really help students to remember and learn new vocabulary.

Teaching tip

Teach pupils to type a word plus 'etymology' into a search engine to find out the original root.

'Etymology' refers to the origin of a word and the historical development of its meaning. Here are some useful words to explore the etymology of.

Word	Origin	Use
Bible	From the Greek τὰ βιβλία *(tà biblía)* meaning 'the books'. See also *biblioteca* (Spanish) and *bibliothèque* (French), meaning 'library'.	What does this tell us about the Bible?
Incarnation	From the Latin *carnis* meaning 'meat' and then *incarnationem*, 'to be made of flesh'.	What do you call an animal that eats meat? What do you call the Texan dish 'chilli with meat'? Therefore the Incarnation is 'God made flesh (meat!)'.
Trinity	From the Latin *trinus* meaning 'threefold, triple'.	What other words linked to the number three can you think of that begin with 'tri'?
Religion	From the Latin *religare* meaning 'to bind', used originally in English to mean 'life under monastic vows'.	What are people bound to?
Islam	From the Arabic اسلام *(islaam)*, meaning 'submission'.	What do Muslims submit to?
Dharma	From the Sanskrit धर्म *(dharma)* meaning 'to hold, maintain, keep', which has developed to refer to 'the law'.	What is it that Hindus maintain or keep?

Learning high-impact quotes

'An apt quotation is like a lamp which flings its light over the whole sentence.' (*Letitia Elizabeth Lando*)

Pupils deserve to leave RE with some quotes stuck in their memory. The ability to quote a key thinker is a significant advantage, not just in an exam, but to help develop students' thinking and debating skills. To be able to quote Jesus, Muhammad or Plato demonstrates key knowledge, and how the quote is used will demonstrate understanding.

Matthew Dell (Senior Lecturer, St Mary's University) suggests this method:

* Identify memorable quotes or 'high-impact' quotes.
* Learn the quotes by rote. This can be tackled in several ways: the whole class repeating the quote, a flash-card approach, or pupils memorising the quote in their heads and then writing it out. Another way is the word-fill approach, where key words in the quote are missing and pupils need to fill them in.
* The rote learning needs to be accompanied with good teaching that unpacks the quote and helps pupils to see the value and significance of the quote.

Once you are committed to enabling all learners to access high-impact quotes, develop a strategic approach. Embed quotes into schemes of work for KS3 so that pupils remember them for KS4. For example, if you are teaching Islam for GCSE, then the Shahadah could be rote learnt in KS3.

> **Bonus idea** ★
>
> Another long-term approach is to select the most important quotes and put them on the walls in the classroom and in corridors (ideally around the school, not just in RE), then take your students on a learning walk five minutes before the end of the lesson to look at the quotes and embed them further in their memory. Ideally, students will remember the quotes far beyond their exams!

Collaborative writing

'When we are writing together, we manage to produce something better than anything we could have written individually.'

Even with unlimited time and resources at their disposal, it can be difficult for some students to write a really good answer or essay. These students might benefit from writing answers collaboratively with others. Even the best students can gain something from the challenge this cooperation requires!

Teaching tip

It's worth developing a bank of model answers from these collaborative answers. They could even be improved on year on year by different classes.

Sort groups

I usually group students by ability, otherwise there is a tendency for the most able students to do the majority of the work in each group. If all students in the group are of a similar ability then they can legitimately challenge one another, in a spirit of cooperation and sometimes competition!

Pick your medium

Are students just planning an essay? If so, a big sheet of paper works well. Giving each student a different-coloured pen can help to easily identify who is contributing and who is not.

If students are writing a long answer or essay, using collaborative software such as Google Docs allows students to edit in real time. You can also check to see who has contributed edits.

A shorter answer could be written by passing a piece of paper back and forth with corrections and improvements. Writing on alternate lines can create the space to do this more easily.

What next?

I'll often give a similar task to students shortly afterwards, where they can apply the skills and knowledge they've picked up from the collaborative writing task.

Word clouds

'I love to use these with students to help them identify the key themes via the reoccurring words.'

It's vital to get students to engage with tricky and often long texts, especially at A level. Sometimes the key themes are obvious, but using word clouds can be a way of making them clear. Word clouds can also be a useful revision prompt to see if students know the texts well enough!

What's a word cloud?

A word cloud or tag cloud is an image composed of words used in a particular document, in which the size of each word indicates its frequency or importance.

Which texts?

You can use this with scripture, for example, one of the Gospels. In a word cloud of Luke's Gospel, words such as 'kingdom', 'sent', 'disciples', 'come', 'ask' and 'answered' all feature prominently. In John's Gospel, the word 'Father' dominates alongside 'one', 'world', 'come' and 'know'.

Word clouds are a great way to summarise and pick out key ideas in A level texts. For example, Ayer's *God-Talk is Evidently Nonsense*, which I've used with every specification I've taught, generates the key words of 'propositions', 'transcendent' and 'existence'.

Teaching tip

Print the word cloud as A4, but in the middle of an A3 sheet. Students can circle or highlight key words and then annotate round the edges.

Bonus idea ★

Word clouds make ideal classroom displays!

'Like' ban

'If I had a pound for every time someone called a synagogue a Jewish church, I'd be retired already.'

It's not surprising that students make links between certain aspects of different religions; however, when they use that phrase 'is like...', it can often be a warning sign that something bad is about to happen!

Taking it further

Obviously there are similarities between, for example, a church and a synagogue, but there are also clear differences! It is useful to get students to identify both.

Here are some key phrases that you can reinforce in order to help students to avoid using 'is like...' all the time:

- place of worship
- holy book
- act of worship
- festival.

For example:

- Your students can replace 'A mosque is like a church for Muslims' with 'A mosque is a place of worship for Muslims'.
- 'The Guru Granth Sahib is like the Sikh Bible' can be replaced with 'The Guru Granth Sahib is the Sikh holy book'.
- 'Puja is like Mass for Hindus' can be replaced with 'Puja is an act of worship for Hindus'.

Ask students why they think religious believers would prefer not using the phrase 'is like...'. If students are believers themselves, they could reverse the common statements for their own religion, for example, 'A church is like a Christian mosque'.

Organise a debate

'Debating represents a long-standing tradition that requires extensive knowledge and an ability to communicate it clearly. It's hugely beneficial for students to do.'

Setting up a debate in the classroom requires careful planning so it is a structured event that doesn't just dissolve into arguing with each other! Debating requires detailed preparation as well as the allocation of roles, and then a final vote or judgement.

The easiest way to set up a classroom debate is as follows:

- Decide on a motion, such as, 'This house believes religious symbols should not be worn at work.' Make sure it is RE-focused!
- Separate the class to do research. Even those not picked as speakers will get the chance to ask questions.
- Allocate roles, for example, a chair, a timekeeper and two teams of four students each.
- The chair introduces and manages the debate.
- The timekeeper monitors the length of the speeches (for instance, three minutes maximum per speech), ringing a bell or similar when time is up.
- The first three speakers each make two or three good points to support or oppose the motion. The final speaker summarises their points and answers any questions posed.

Allow the debate to flow as much as possible. It can be useful for you or a nominated student (or group of students) to provide individual feedback to those on the debate teams. At the end of the debate, a vote to see if the motion passes or fails is a fun way to finish.

Teaching tip

There are lots of ways to set up debates! This is my preferred model for the classroom.

Taking it further

If students enjoy debating then a lunchtime debate club can be popular, and can help to raise the profile of the department. There are also competitions locally and nationally to join in with. If this is led by the RE department, it can be great publicity for the good work that goes on in classrooms daily!

Speed debating

'I had to think really quickly and move from one topic to another; I didn't want any awkward silences!'

Getting students to challenge one another verbally can be a good way to energise a class before tackling an exam question or writing an essay. Try this twist on speed dating!

Taking it further

Students can practise their evaluation skills by taking sides on a statement or question while sitting in rows this way. For example, you could pick one row to argue *for* and the other side *against* the final question.

Sit students in two rows facing each other. One row will move places and the other will stay stationary; as a student gets to the end of the row, they walk round and join back on the other end. This allows students to move along and speak to a number of others.

Give students a set amount of time to talk to each other about a question you give them before they move on to the next person for the next question. One minute works well for KS3 and GCSE classes, but longer periods work well at A level. Break the topic area down into sections. Here is an example on the features of a mosque:

- What is a mosque? (One minute.)
- What is a _____? (One minute.)
  Suggestions: minaret, ablutions area, prayer hall, mihrab, minbar, dome.
- Final question: do you think it is important for Muslims to pray in the mosque? (Perhaps two minutes.)

You can use this activity to lead into getting students to answer an exam question or essay question. This may be similar to the final question you give in the debate.

Silent debating

'The students who never put their hand up in class were more than happy to get involved when they needed to write their contributions.'

Discussion and debate are common features of the RE classroom, and can be highly effective. Yet some students lack confidence and are very reluctant participants. Changing the medium of the debate can enable greater participation.

Consider the following in advance:

Debate size: this activity works effectively in pairs, fours and larger groups (such as ten A level students).

Resources: each group will need a large piece of paper, though some teachers forgo this and just ask students to write on the tables themselves (make sure the writing will wipe off afterwards!). A collection of different-coloured pens helps everyone to see who wrote what.

Key question: I usually pick a controversial statement to evaluate. You could allocate 'sides' in advance, perhaps giving students time to do some advance preparation. Write the statement in the middle of each piece of paper.

Students then 'debate' the statement, taking it in turns to write (with only one student writing at a time). The others read and consider their responses. Start by moving around the group in order (later you may choose to have a free for all!). Encourage students to draw lines and arrows to connect different ideas and indicate lines of reasoning.

Teaching tip

A silent debate can be great preparation for an essay question.

Taking it further

Another approach is to turn this into a carousel activity. If you have different questions being debated by each smaller group, at a certain point, students could move to the next table/question and add to that one too.

Assessment

Part 10

Breaking down the mark scheme

'I want to peer assess, but my students can't understand the mark scheme.'

Despite there being just two Assessment Objectives (AOs) for GCSE and A level, the statements used can be hard to decipher for students. This activity is a good way to get students engaged with the mark scheme in an accessible way.

Let's start with a three-levelled AO1 question. When you read the complex statements on the mark schemes, you can often work out what students need to focus on. For example:

- **Knowledge:** narrow (L1), range (L2), wide range (L3).
- **Understanding:** superficial (L1), developing depth (L2), deep (L3).
- **Accuracy:** inaccuracies (L1), some inaccuracies (L2), accurate (L3).

This truncated version of the mark scheme can easily be set out in a tick-box format. Class discussion may be valuable, for example: 'For this question, what is the expected range of knowledge?'

When students want to mark an answer, they can use the tick-box mark scheme to identify their strengths and weaknesses easily. For example, putting a tick against each of the three categories might result in a conclusion such as 'My work was accurate (L3) and showed depth (L3), but didn't have a good enough range of information (L2).'

This can make self- and peer-marking far more meaningful. It can also help students to understand what is limiting their answer.

Collecting exercise books

'Why did no one ever tell me this? This will genuinely change my life!'

RE teachers always need to look for time-saving measures when marking. Here are a few ways to help you stay on top of marking by thinking about how and when you collect books.

Always open: ask students to either find the last page where their book was marked, or the specific page you want to mark, and collect the books opened like this. This can save a significant amount of time, rather than you opening each book and trying to find the right page.

Order: if you need to enter marks into your planner or mark book, get the first student on the register to collect the books in order. Provide them with a list (though after a few occasions they will no doubt remember the order!). You could always speed this up by having two lists and asking the last student on the register to start from the other end.

Take ten: if you have a school or department policy about the regularity of marking, work out the minimum number of books you need to take each lesson to prevent yourself from being faced with a daunting pile of a complete class set to mark! For example, you could take seven or eight books a week, and over four weeks mark the full set.

Timetable it: work out the ideal schedule for collecting and returning books, to give yourself the maximum time and/or PPA time to mark each set. Careful planning on this can avoid overburdening yourself on certain days or weeks.

> **Bonus idea** ★
>
> Factor in some 'admin time' for your students before collecting books. Get them to do all the underlining, gluing in, ensuring homework is in the correct place, etc. It may save you having to do it for them!

Marking for lots of classes

'I teach more classes than anyone else in the school. In fact, I teach the whole of KS3!'

The RE teacher can often have a disproportionately high number of classes and as a result, the marking load can be significant. Here are some strategies to help with this.

Teaching tip

Keep your own exercise book for each class you teach and jot down where you have got to in the lesson so you don't get confused between classes. They can also be used for live modelling if you have a visualiser!

Marking grids: these are tick sheets that contain a list of progressively challenging criteria. You can add these to students' work, ticking the boxes for criteria they have fulfilled (with their target being focused on criteria they have not fulfilled). Students can write their own WWW ('what went well') and EBI ('even better if') if required.

Stamps or stickers: if you often end up writing the same comments, purchasing a stamp or finding a way of printing these comments onto sticky labels can be time-saving. For example, I have a sticky label to help mark the presentation of students' work; it includes categories such as 'underline the title' and 'include the date' that just require a tick.

Carry forward feedback: students take their target from their most recent similar task and write it at the top of the page before starting their next task. For example, 'add a source of wisdom or authority' or 'add more key terms'. Before they hand the task in to be marked, they have to highlight on their answer where they have met their target. (To make this process flow, it helps to set at least two similar tasks – such as two 12-mark exam questions – back to back.)

Getting students to choose their own WWW and EBI: make a list of WWW and EBI on a whole-class feedback sheet as you read a set of books. Students then have to choose the feedback that matches their work.

Multiple-choice questions

'The use of multiple-choice questions, especially with my many classes, has revolutionised plenaries, homework and planning.'

Too often, multiple-choice questions have been considered not to be 'higher order' (something RE always prides itself on). However, without key knowledge, it's impossible to progress in the subject. When written well, multiple-choice questions allow the teacher to work out the level of understanding of individuals or the class.

A few tips for creating a multiple-choice quiz:

- Ensure you clearly identify what it is you want to test students on. Don't just write questions for the sake of it!
- Plan out in advance what each question will cover so you get a good spread for the desired number of questions (for example, I use ten questions to cover two specification points at GCSE).
- Devise four plausible answers for each question. (If you create a 'silly' answer then it's almost not worth adding!)
- Use an online platform for your quiz (such as Google Forms). This has the great added benefit that it will self-mark students' answers. Depending on the platform you use, you can also shuffle the order of the answers (or even the questions).
- Keep it low stakes. Sometimes it's even worth students just doing the quizzes without you recording how well they did.

Teaching tip

Consider making one of the answer options 'I don't know' or similar. Some teachers find this helpful rather than just allowing students to randomly guess if they really don't know the answer.

Taking it further

Up the stakes! Try ascribing points to the answers (such as +5 for the correct answer, -5 for an incorrect answer). This could be used in combination with the 'I don't know' option to help avoid guessing.

An example question

How is the Promised Land described in Exodus 3:8?

- As the Kingdom of the Jews.
- Like the Garden of Eden.
- Flowing with milk and honey.
- A place of joy and happiness.

Good homework

'I only see my class once a week, so I need to ensure what I set them is effective.'

The real question when it comes to homework is whether it's useful and effective. This is especially true in RE, when time is always short. What makes for 'good' homework in RE?

For me, the best homework fits into one of three categories:

- **Applying:** practice (possibly of exam questions), completing structured class work, or further tasks that extend or deepen learning.
- **Further reading and comprehension:** reading is always useful! However, understanding needs to be checked via questioning.
- **Learning:** this means that information is consolidated and embedded in memory. This may be learning factual information, such as key words, dates, or scholar names.

Try not to set:

- **Elaborate construction projects:** where students spend more time doing non-RE tasks than RE. This can be a waste of time and resources. Are there better ways to learn about a mosque than building one out of biscuits?
- **Vague research:** if a student gives you a printout from Wikipedia, footnotes and all, you know you haven't set a good homework task. Setting key questions to answer about a topic easily gets around this (and may only take a few minutes more to set!).
- **Inappropriate computer-based tasks:** for example, making a PowerPoint presentation may not be possible for some students outside of school.

Socratic questioning

'The unexamined life is not worth living.' (*Socrates*)

The Socratic questioning method is useful for all teachers but feels particularly apt for RE teachers.

The Socratic method is said to be the foundation of critical thinking, and if RE is not critical then it's not of much use at all! It's regarded as one of the oldest teaching methods, but also one of the most effective. Even today, the skill of questioning is often a key factor in assessing teacher performance. The Socratic method focuses on providing more questions than answers, but this helps students to come to logical conclusions about the topic in hand.

Teaching tip

Students could take the 'hot seat' and be quizzed by their peers. You might start with students working in pairs or small groups, but with practice, some individuals will grow in confidence and be ready to take the 'hot seat' in front of the class!

There are six main focuses for questions:

Clarifying concepts	Probing implications and consequences
• What exactly does this mean? • Can you give me an example? • How does this relate to the topic?	• Do these claims make sense? • Are they desirable? • How do these claims fit with...? • What are the consequences of that?
Probing assumptions • If this is correct, what else could we assume? • What would happen if...?	**Questioning viewpoints and perspectives** • Who benefits from this claim? • Why is it better than...? • Why is it different from...?
Probing rationale, reasons and evidence • Why is that happening? • What evidence is there to support what you are saying?	**Questioning the question** • Why do you think I asked this question? • What does that mean?

Retrieval roulette

'Adam Boxer has created a tool that's useful for all subjects, but I've found it's worked really well in GCSE RS.'

'Retrieval practice' is a technical name for quizzing or testing past material, and is proven to be one of the most effective memory techniques. Teachers have become more systematic in this, ensuring students more regularly go back over previous material to help remember it better. Adam Boxer's 'retrieval roulette' is a very helpful aid in this.

Teaching tip

Adam's original spreadsheet (as well as many different iterations for different subjects) can be accessed from his blog: https://achemicalorthodoxy.wordpress.com/resources

Taking it further

Do you recap learning from previous years? For example, do you test Year 9 on Year 7 or 8 content? A very clear and systematic system for retrieval, using principles of interleaving, could do this.

It's easy to test prior learning by quizzing key words, scholars, quotes, etc. But how systematic is this? Do you keep a record? The science teacher Adam Boxer devised a useful Excel spreadsheet (called the 'retrieval roulette') that uses a list of questions and answers to generate a random ten-question quiz. Using it in its original format, you can set it to ask five questions from any point in the course and five questions from the current topic.

Obviously, to produce the questions in the first place takes substantial time and effort. However, this can be done as a department (or even by a group of teachers virtually if you are doing the same specification). Some teachers have got able Year 11 students to write questions, and then just checked and tidied them.

A. J. Smith compares retrieval practice to the recap at the start of an episode on TV: a brief recap is useful and prompts deeper and wider thinking about the plot and characters. It's a prompt to the memories of previous episodes. If questions are picked carefully, they can also make links to the current lesson.

The retrieval roulette can provide the ideal starter to all lessons, so the investment in the short term really does pay off in the long term.

Revision and exam skills

Part 11

Effective revision in RE

'Understanding something in the moment is most definitely not the same as remembering something!'

GCSE and A level RS demand that students know a lot of information! It's also true that students are often not very good at using 'generic revision skills' across the board. Ensure you spend some time explaining what good revision is in RE.

When it comes to improving your students' revision skills, here are the key points to share.

Most effective techniques for revising:

- **Practice of exam or test questions:** do students have a bank of questions prepared by the teacher? Have they been shown how to access exam board questions? Other testing could include knowledge recall quizzes, or multiple choice quizzes, rather than exam questions.
- **Distributed practice (returning to topics over a longer period of time):** how are Year 10 topics revisited during Year 11? You could do this via homework tasks.

Moderately effective techniques for revising:

- **Interleaved practice:** teach students to chunk and mix up topics by doing, for example, the Trinity, the nature of Allah, and Christian literature.
- **Elaborative interrogation:** this involves pupils working in pairs and challenging one another, or reviewing their exercise books and writing 'Why?' against key pieces of information... and then answering!
- **Self-explanation:** how do you link previous information to new information?

Less effective techniques include: summarisation, simple highlighting or underlining, and rereading.

The RE escape room

'I needed to do something to get my students more enthused about revision lessons. Using the "escape room" format has been hugely popular!'

RE teacher Abbey Elton created an 'escape room' lesson for her GCSE students and shared it online. This became hugely popular and many teachers have used the format for their exam classes to generate excitement about their revision.

The format of the lesson works like this:

- Students must work in groups of around six and be seated together. Each group can come up with their own team name.
- Groups are given a variety of tasks to complete. Once a group has completed all tasks set, they're allowed to 'escape' the room and leave the lesson! These can be carefully constructed to test different parts of the course, including short-answer quizzes, key scholar overviews, key-word tests, picture challenges, planning exam-question answers, etc.
- Groups have to complete each task fully and have it checked by you in order to start the next task.
- Only one person in each group is allowed to come up to find out if their task has been successfully completed.
- Students can use notes and textbooks to help them, but they can't speak to different groups or they'll be given a time penalty.

If you've ever been to an escape room yourself, you'll know what this is based on. (If not, perhaps a department night out?)

> **Taking it further**
>
> Could your students plan an escape room for one another? Just the planning of this is helpful for learning!

Being critical

'Despite using a clear essay structure, my students were still missing opportunities to critically evaluate.'

RE students often seem to love listening to or telling a good story. However, at both GCSE and A level, this can result in them describing information in such a way that they do not pick up on the key marks for analysis and evaluation. Yet with some clear direction, students can be given the ability to transform descriptive sentences.

Teaching tip

Get students to reread work before handing it in, to add in phrases at points where they have missed an opportunity to evaluate. This could be a good way of peer assessing: what are the missed opportunities in this work?

Bonus idea ★

Why not create a bank of good evaluative language to share? Words could include correctly/incorrectly, usefully/unhelpfully, accurately/inaccurately, justified/unjustified, etc.

One way to make students' writing less descriptive is by using the 'JQR' approach, suggested by Arabella Saunders, an RE teacher.

- **Judgement:** use evaluative language.
- **Question:** link back to the language of the question.
- **Reason:** explain a specific reason for your judgement.

For example, if students were to answer the question 'Evaluate the claim that Christianity should be completely abandoned', it would not be uncommon to see statements such as: 'Sigmund Freud starts off by describing religion as an illusion.' However, with a few small tweaks using the JQR method, it could be transformed:

'Sigmund Freud is <u>correct</u> to describe religion as an illusion. Therefore, **the claim that Christianity should be completely abandoned** is <u>sensible</u> *for the wellbeing of individuals and society*.'

Here the underlining indicates the judgement. The text in bold is the linking back to the question. The text in italics is the reasoning.

This is an excellent way to start each paragraph in an essay and ensure that judgement is not simply left to the final conclusion.

Elaborate and develop

'What's my favourite word? "Because."'

Students need to ensure that factual information is then transformed into developed points in their writing. Asking questions that will prompt them to elaborate can help with this.

RE is a complex subject that can rarely rely on simple answers! Answers will usually need to be justified and explained. *Why* do Hindus believe in reincarnation? *How* does a Buddhist reach enlightenment? Asking questions such as 'why' and 'how' can provide a great challenge when trying to move to extended writing.

However, students may find it hard to know exactly which information they should elaborate on. For example, when they're writing an answer to an exam question, they may 'develop the point' but not in a way that adds marks to their response.

An example two-mark exam question might be: 'Why do Christians believe in the Trinity?' One student answer is: 'Reference to the Father, Son and Holy Spirit is found in the Creed. **This is a statement of Christian beliefs said publicly.**' Here the bit in bold is factually correct, but doesn't actually develop the answer in relation to the question. A better answer would be: 'Reference to the Father, Son and Holy Spirit is found in the Creed, **which is a statement that was formulated by early Christians to ensure shared beliefs.**' This demonstrates history and origin rather than just current usage.

Questions you can ask to help students include:

- What does this mean?
- Can you give an example?
- What backs this up?
- What is the implication of this?
- Which argument is most convincing?

Teaching tip

The use of 'why?' and 'how?' when marking students' work, especially their class notes, can force them to elaborate their answers.

Bonus idea ★

Why not create a bank of connectives that can be used regularly? Some teachers produce desk mats with phrases and ideas to help develop points in a simple and effective way, while others print these out and put them on the front or back of exercise books.

Cornell note-taking

'The best note-taking system in the world?'

Many successful students, as well as business people, have found that the Cornell note-taking system is a very effective way to record lessons in a way that is highly organised and useful for regular review.

With the high level of content at GCSE and A level, Cornell note-taking is an ideal technique to use. It's also a great way to encourage regular reviewing of material, and provides an easy way for students to self-test.

During the lesson, students fill in the 'Lesson notes' section, as directed by their teacher. They complete the 'Cues' and the 'Summary box' sections after the lesson. When revising a topic, students can cover up the lesson notes and use the cues and the summary as prompts.

Title and date	
Cues • Key words • Dates • Names • Books • Questions	**Lesson notes**
Summary box	

Try to discourage students from writing their summary boxes during the lesson. Ideally, they will revisit their notes to complete each section separately, which will mean they have to revisit the material several times.

Explaining the exam

'Too often students see one or two words of the question and then just answer the question they hope is there!'

As subject experts, we can quickly assess the exact demands of exam questions, but students often don't. Therefore, it's important to share your thinking process with them.

Some schools do 'walking talking mocks', taking students into the exam hall to 'talk through' the exam. I prefer to do this in the classroom.

Live explanations

Students could have the exam paper in front of them, while you use a visualiser to project your annotations of the exam paper in real time. Show them a variety of questions – especially those that look similar at face value but are actually asking quite different things, for example, 'What happens at Passover?' vs 'Why is Passover important?'

Prepared explanations

If you spend time looking at the exam paper in advance, you can underline, annotate, highlight, explain and suggest on the paper *before* it's photocopied and shared. Students then have your thinking shared with them as they attempt to answer the questions.

In the long run, this hopefully gets students to think more carefully about the questions before they launch in. It can also help them to develop good techniques for their own annotations. It's not something to do frequently and it is time-consuming. However, I, like many others, have got better results simply by doing this and not providing any more knowledge. Therefore it's clear that students throw away marks by not using what they know!

> **Taking it further**
>
> As students get more confident, they could explain question types, common errors or misconceptions on the exam paper to their peers. This obviously only works in the classroom, not so much in the hall!

Specification checklist

'As much as I try to follow the scheme of work, the nature of RE means we end up jumping around a little bit. Have I covered all of the specification?'

Despite careful planning, especially during A level (but also GCSE), lessons can end up being taught in a slightly different order. Lessons can also get missed due to staff or student absences, trips, and so on. It's vital to have a way to record what's been covered from the specification, and students can be empowered with this information.

Teaching tip

A useful revision activity is to give a copy of the full specification to students and ensure they can define every key word on it!

Taking it further

Why not display the specification checklists around the department or email them to parents? Simply having a copy of it in students' books is sometimes not enough!

Exam specifications are easily found online, and could simply be printed and ticked off by students. However, I've found that they can be better used for spaced practice (breaking practice up into short sessions) and ensuring further review of topics.

GCSE

There's a vast amount of content for students to cover at GCSE. Highlighting the benefit of repeated and spaced practice is really useful for students. Creating a checklist that has each specification point and then five review points can help students to plan their revision. If you have online and/or multiple-choice quizzes linked to each topic, these can be recorded on the checklist.

A level

Alongside the specification points on a checklist, I find it useful to then have three columns: class notes, extra reading notes and the knowledge organiser. Students can tick class notes if they can find them, tick for extra reading evidence and tick when the knowledge organiser is done; they can also date them too. It may also be useful to have a second checklist similar to the GCSE one to map out review points.

Writing RE exam questions

'My students could write questions, but when they actually looked at the specification, they realised they didn't work!'

Getting students to write questions for you, with a clear focus on the specification, can help them to understand exactly what could and couldn't be asked in the exam.

Here's a made-up specification point for an Islam GCSE syllabus: 'The pillar of Shahadah: its nature, role and significance for Sunni and Shi'a Muslims; include reference to Qur'an Surah 3:18; why it is important to recite and how it is used today.'

It's then useful to give students a question type, for example, 'Explain...' (4 marks) or 'Evaluate...' (12 marks). This might lead to questions such as:

The process of writing questions, swapping questions to answer, and then peer marking can be useful as part of a revision session or a plenary.

- 'Explain the role of the Shahadah for Sunni and Shi'a Muslims.' (Good – it covers the specification point 'its... role... for Sunni and Shi'a Muslims'.)
- 'Explain the history of the Shahadah.' (Bad – the history of the Shahadah isn't mentioned in the specification.)
- '"It is important for Muslims to recite the Shahadah." Evaluate this claim.' (Good – it covers the specification point 'why it is important to recite'.)
- '"Muslims need to follow the Five Pillars." Evaluate this claim.' (Bad – this specification point is only talking about the Shahadah, not the other four pillars.)

This really helps students to focus on the wording and language of the question, which should help them to focus their answers in the exam. (Is the question asking about the role of the Shahadah, its importance, or how it is used?)

Bonus idea ★

Get students to write a mark scheme to go with their questions.

Live marking

'I find it useful to talk students through my thought process as I'm marking a piece of work.'

Live marking is an effective way of supporting students in preparation for exams.

Live marking can be very time-consuming, but a good use of time! Don't leave this until the last five minutes of a lesson as it can often take up a significant part of a lesson.

Show your students an exam question that you're going to mark for them. If you have access to a visualiser, you can present your students with an answer you've written – for example, a paragraph of text. Go through it sentence by sentence, explaining what you are looking for as your mark. Show them your thinking in real time!

As students get familiar with this process, you can ask for input from them. Or you could ask students to rewrite the answer you've shown them based on the marking you've just done.

Using exemplar answers

'I can write a model answer, but I don't know how to use it in class!'

Students are always asking for model answers, and they're a really useful tool at GCSE and A level. However, the challenge is always about getting students to actively use them rather than just trying to copy them! What useful things can they get from an exemplar answer?

Nikki McGee, RE teacher and Head of Philosophy, Religion and Ethics, suggests four key things to do when providing a student with a model or exemplar answer. It's useful to hand an exemplar answer to students at the same time as returning a piece of their own work. Then:

- They have to highlight key things on the exemplar answer such as key terms, technical vocabulary, scholars and quotes.
- They will have been set a target on their own essay, such as 'add counter-arguments'. On the exemplar answer, they have to show where it demonstrates the skills that their own essay was lacking. They then have to redraft their own essay using the exemplar answer as a model.
- They have to identify on the exemplar answer a piece of subject knowledge they didn't know, which would have improved their own essay.
- They have to identify something in the exemplar answer related to exam technique that they want to steal, such as using connectives or using sentences at the end of a paragraph to link back to the question.

Teaching tip

For shorter exam questions, why not write an exemplar answer while students are writing theirs, displaying yours once they have finished?

Agree or disagree?

'My students either agree or disagree. Nothing in between! I need a tool to help them in preparation for exams.'

There is often difficulty in getting students to fully evaluate and analyse critically. Learning the subtleties of disagreement or agreement needs to be taught for most. Visual tools can help with this.

Moving around the room

Some teachers like to get students out of their seats to show the range of their opinions. This may work well if you have a decent amount of space. One end of the room could be 'agree' and the other 'disagree', then students have to pick a spot to stand in the room that reflects to what extent they 'agree' or 'disagree' with a statement. You could start with less controversial statements or questions before moving on to trickier ones. It's important to get students to justify where they are standing and why!

Agree-o-meter

These have been produced for a variety of subjects online. They often have a statement or claim at the top of a page, followed by a diagram that looks like a speedometer (with markers on it such as 'agree', 'partly agree', 'partly disagree' and 'disagree' – or perhaps instead, smiles moving through to frowns!). Students decide where on the speedometer their opinion lies, providing evidence to back this up.

Vocabulary building

Try getting students to add these words to 'I agree...' and 'I disagree...': 'totally', 'strongly', 'to some extent', and 'slightly'.